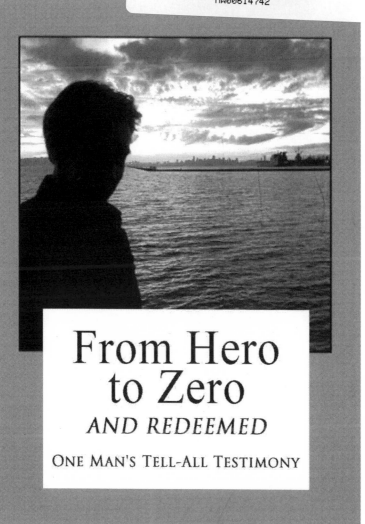

From Hero to Zero

AND REDEEMED

ONE MAN'S TELL-ALL TESTIMONY

Eric Soldahl

Dearest Hal,

Thought you may enjoy a few sections of the Book, as I write about the folks, Center St. area and TAHOE too! Best to your son & family, HUGS, ERIC

From Hero to Zero: And Redeemed - A Testimony

Copyright © 2019 Eric Alan Soldahl

Dovestar Publishing International
55-300 Firestone, La Quinta CA 92253

ISBN-13: 978-1732024625
ISBN-10: 1732024626
ISBN -10 for Kindle: 978-1-7320246-3-2

Published in the United States of America. 2019   2nd Edition

Some names have been changed to honor privacy.

Scripture taken from the Holy Bible, NIV, NKJV, NRSV,

All rights reserved.

Cover photo was taken by my wife, Elizabeth. It is a cell phone snap of my "silhouette at sunset," overlooking the San Francisco skyline; near a favorite sailing spot.

Order Books on Amazon.com

Contact information:
ericsoldahl@gmail.com
Website: www.faithonfire.net

BISAC: Biography & Autobiography/Christian Living/Men/Faith
$9.95 USD

What Readers are Saying:

"This faithful and poignant account is a book with clear inner messages, expressed so boldly and candidly. I was so drawn into Eric's honest retelling of his life: obsessed with work, women and the battle of the bottle; and how God's love in essence saved him."

-T.K. Ireland

"This is an enlightening book and its content kept me from being able to put it down. I ended up reading the whole book in one sitting..."

James Farmer, Ph.D./Author/Musician

"There's something for everyone in this heartfelt story; with family dynamics, travel, sports, music, politics, business, health and faith. Totally inspirational and something I would highly recommend for men and those seeking to understand true sanctification."

Bob Litchfield, ThD

Dedication

Thanks *to my Heavenly Father* who gave encouragement and inspiration to pen these pages.

Dedicated to: *My amazing wife, Elizabeth, who is my heart.*

In Honor of my faithful brother, Daniel Soldahl 1952-2009, who taught me perseverance by example.

Special thanks for editing help and read-throughs to: Elizabeth, Courtney Artiste, Mom Florence, Heather Bowers and our three sons: Grayson, Nolan and Paul.

"Trust in the Lord with all of your heart and lean not on your own understanding; In all your ways acknowledge Him and He will make straight your paths."

(Proverbs 3:5-6)

Preface

As a young boy, two stories always captivated me; The Prodigal Son and Jonah and the Whale. I was the younger brother in real life and often found myself fleeing. As my journey unfolded, there was a struggle: "To whom do I belong? God or the world?" At midlife, I read *The Return of the Prodigal Son:* I could continue adrift on the ocean, at the mercy of its waves, or take the *Road Less Traveled*. My hope in writing *From Hero to Zero* is to encourage men who have had similar battles in life. May you be renewed in faith, or find needed redemption; whether an obedient son, or one coming home.

Love & Peace, *Eric Soldahl*

Introduction

I was always running in my life. Running from truth; Busy at work. And busy trying to make things work out at home. My life was consumed by business, music and family.

Approaching middle age around the year 2000, I was a single dad with young children feeling overwhelmed. After some success in real estate and music, the hard times had hit. Lost marriages, custody battles, foreclosure and now even my longtime band had split up. Through the years I had not been faithful to my true calling. There were many years of seeking fame, fortune, and females.

I had worked on multi-million dollar business deals and shared stages with famous musicians. But now I was lost. At mid-life I found myself with a broken life. *A broken heart.*

Starting over, I moved from Nevada to Paradise, California to be closer to my children and aging parents. I quit traveling in the popular music world leaving the concert circuit, casino lights, and the all-night recording sessions behind.

On New Year's Day, as the new century dawned, I prayed for the first time in years:

Please God, I just need enough to pay my child support.

The next day a man called from out of the blue with a music job for a Calvary Lutheran church. I had grown up in a Lutheran Church, often playing piano.

1

"You will be forming a choir and leading the worship team," the Church President said.

The monthly pay was exactly the same as my child support! I took notice. I was being asked to lead music and the church choir, but over the years, I had been no "choir boy," myself.

"Yes—look forward to meeting you," I said, "I want the job."

Soon I was directing worship and playing piano, guitar and organ at three services each week.

"It's been a while since doing music in church," I told the choir members. *Hope I stay on track*, I thought.

Hope they don't find out about my past…

Man in the Camel Hair Coat

A tall slender man with long stringy hair sauntered down the center aisle towards the front of the Calvary Church. He donned a long camel hair coat and held a walking cane with an eagle mounted on top. Striking features—mid-thirties, but appearing much older at the same time.

Others watched as he slid close to me in the empty front pew. I was hesitant to look up at the man. But then I saw his translucent eyes. There was a calm—peace like I have never felt before. We sat quietly side-by-side. I had just been hired as the new music director at the church. He signaled for something to write on. Someone from the row behind us handed me a yellow guest card. The man smiled as I passed the card to him.

Then the man in the camel coat wrote several indescribable words in what looked like an ancient script.

3

Was this Hebrew or Aramaic? Was this man homeless? A Prophet? The man nodded and handed me the message. *The following moments would change my life forever...*

Innocent Days

I was born in Minneapolis, Minnesota at Northwestern Hospital, on a sub-zero morning. My first cry was during a time of innocence. It was in the middle of the fifties. Elvis ruled the airwaves and James Dean the movie box office.

The story goes that a nurse held me up and proclaimed, "This one came out singing."

My childhood was filled with sledding through icy winters with our family of five. My favorite winter activity was going downhill on our big wooden toboggan.

One of my first memories was catching a fish through a hole in the ice. Along with uncles and cousins, we learned to fish from a "tiny house," heated by a fire, on a frozen lake.

Another time, my brother, Danny and I built an Igloo out of ice in our front yard. My sister, Nancy, started to move her dolls and clothes into the ice house. I packed my underwear.

There was a bedtime story every night. Dad's favorite story was one he made up about, "Little Ever Ever." The main character in the story would always end up living, "forever and ever," in heaven. I loved books and stories. My older brother and sister taught me to read at a young age.

Every Sunday, we dressed up for the Central Lutheran Church in Minneapolis; reminiscent of a large cathedral in Europe. Watching my big brother, in the Boys' Choir, I longed to be up there with him singing. After church, we often dined at one of the grandparent's homes.

One Sunday, after turning four, I rushed into the kitchen where everyone was sitting down for dinner.

"Come quick! I just saw Jesus in the clouds!"

I grabbed my siblings' sleeves and led them to my bedroom window. There, out the window, we saw the face of Jesus floating by in a cloud. The three of us were in silent awe. Then the cloud disappeared; the adults missed it.

Often, in times of trouble, I have drawn on that face of Jesus in a single cloud smiling down on me. A few weeks later after church, Mom says I sat at Grandma's grand piano singing, *Jesus Loves Me,* playing with both hands.

That night at dinner, my parents talked about saving enough money to buy a piano someday.

Dressed for Church in Minnesota, Age 5

I loved all sports; anything with a ball. With sports, as in life, Dad instilled in us kids to root for the underdog.

My brother and I joined the Waite Park Hockey Team and the YMCA program called "Indian Guides." One time a totem pole fell on my brother's head and he had to have several stiches.

"I didn't push it over," I said, while dressed in my Indian headdress. Later, during a spanking, I cried: "It was an accident!" My life would become filled with, "accidents."

Grandma Soldahl consoled me, "God is always with you."

"Even when I'm in trouble?"

"Especially when you're in trouble." Gram took my hand and led me to the piano where she played her favorite hymn.

6

Travels with Family

Many of our summers were spent exploring the *Ten Thousand Lakes*, in Minnesota. As a teacher, Dad had summers off from work. We enjoyed cabins and boating on Green Lake, or canoeing up the Gunflint Trail. There were the large statues of Paul Bunyan, the fabled logger and his blue ox. Dad had been a logger one season; "Hardest job in the world," he said.

My parents did a great job showing us children a sampling of Canada and the United States. One fall we traveled through Quebec and Montreal to Niagara Falls and New York City, where we saw the Macy's Thanksgiving Day Parade. It was a real splurge to eat at *The Tavern on the Green*, in Central Park, one of the best known restaurants in the world.

On Broadway we saw the musicals *Camelot* and *The Music Man*. Afterward, Dad bought both records and played them endlessly.

On one family excursion to Washington D.C., the folks took us through the White House while John Fitzgerald Kennedy was President—tours were welcomed then. It was called, "a Season in Camelot."

Our tour guide reported, "JFK loves to put on a record of the Camelot musical each evening."

"We saw the Camelot show in New York!" I said. Then tugging on the sleeve of our guide, I asked a final question: "Can I meet the President?"

"Stay Quiet"

One fun-filled vacation to Mt. Rushmore was cut short after my sister, Nancy, became gravely ill. It had started with strep throat. After several tests, she was diagnosed with a serious case of rheumatic fever.

Over the following weeks, we were asked to, *"Stay quiet,"* and keep away from Nan's bedroom.

One day I snuck into her room and apologized for cutting off her Barbie Doll's hair. I thought she might die, and I wanted to confess to her. That Christmas, the folks gave Nan a professional art set. She produced cheerful paintings from her gloomy room. Finally, the rheumatic fever subsided and Nan would survive. Nan had been confined for nearly a year.

A Year in Kent, Ohio

In 1962, our family moved from Minneapolis to Kent, Ohio where the folks thought the weather would be warmer; especially as my sister was regaining strength. But the hot Midwestern summer brought unexpected weather.

It was exciting when a thunderstorm headed in our direction. "Come on!" Dan would say, running outside. Dan taught me how to count the seconds from the lightning flash to the time the thunder struck. He could even tell the direction of a storm.

One balmy day, a tornado headed straight for us.

My nine-year-old brother ran from the corn field across the street, throwing corn kernels in the air tracking the direction of the funnel cloud. Then Mom called out through the kitchen window, for us to come inside.

Without time for our playmates to run home, many of the neighborhood children ran into our basement for safety.

Gleefully, we sang songs while the storm raged. Then Mom told the story about *Jonah and the Whale*. Jonah ran away from what God wanted him to do. In a big storm, Jonah ended up inside the belly of the whale.

"We're like Jonah hiding in the belly of the basement!" my big brother called out.

"*Why did he run away?*" I wondered.

After a year in Kent Ohio, my Dad felt a change of climate was needed. Later that decade, four students were shot during protests at Kent State near where we lived. So we bought a *Farmer's Almanac* to find the sunniest town in America. It was called Castro Valley.

"If we wanted weather like this, we could have stayed in Minnesota," Mom said.

"Castro Valley or Bust"

On the final leg of our journey west, we approached our new home. Nan made a cardboard sign that read: "Castro Valley or Bust!"

Soon, we were waving the sign out the back window of our green 1962 Chevy station wagon driving up the steep Altamont pass in California. The engine sputtered under the weight of a U-Haul with all our worldly possessions. Suddenly, we heard the car muffler scraping the asphalt and sparks were flying from under the wagon. Dad pulled carefully to the side of the highway and I heard him swear for the first time.

A few minutes later, an old man in a pickup truck came by, "Need a ride?" he asked.

My siblings and I climbed into the back of the open pickup. Mom and Dad hopped into the cab. The driver sped to over eighty miles an hour down the winding old highway. Our driver grabbed a beer and popped a can open. Mom began praying.

"He's driving his age," my brother said.

"He must be a hundred!" I said.

After the truck slowed down outside Livermore, we settled in at a cheap motel.

"It will take a week to fix the wagon," Dad said, after talking with a mechanic at the service station next door.

"I don't mind a bit," I replied, "this motel has a swimming pool and a soda pop machine."

Dan said, "Hey, can I have a quarter for this bed? It's one of those *Magic Fingers Vibrating Beds*!"

On our first week in Castro Valley, we felt a jolt and then our new home rocked back and forth.

"Earthquake!" my brother said, sounded excited.

Thinking fast, Dad responded with humor, "Let's get down on the floor and put our ears to the ground, where we can hear it better!"

The Times They are a Changin'

Elementary Troubles

It was tough being the new third grader, at Vannoy Elementary, in Castro Valley. That October, the Cuban Missile Crisis alarmed the world. The Russians were deploying nuclear weapons to the small Cuban island near the United States.

My teacher scolded me when I asked if Cuba's communist dictator, Fidel Castro, was from Castro Valley.

Every afternoon for a month, we were given drill instructions by Mrs. Willis on how to survive a nuclear blast:

"Stay away from the windows—no talking—hide under your desk!" We were further instructed to hold our head between our legs.

"So you can kiss your 'you-know-what' goodbye," my friend, Daryl Strom said, while making kissing sounds to the nervous girls.

That November in 1963, the innocence of America would further be lost, when President John F. Kennedy was shot and killed in Dallas. On a dark and cloudy November morning, my fourth grade teacher, Mr. Gosset, rolled a little black and white TV into the classroom. We watched the horrific events unfold before us. My teacher began crying.

That day we were excused by Principal Miller with the mandate to, "Go home immediately without stopping."

On the way home from Vannoy, my bright new friend, Paul Pappas remarked, "Vice President, Johnson, is from Texas. Kennedy was shot in Texas—makes you kind of wonder…" he finished. A few days later I watched on live TV as Kennedy's suspected assassin, Lee Harvey Oswald was shot and killed.

A New President

That summer of '64 we returned to Minnesota for a visit. My Aunt Mary Martha was a campaign manager for Lyndon Banes Johnson. "LBJ" was running for President after Kennedy was shot. We were invited to a gathering in St. Paul where our family would meet Vice President Humphrey and hear President Johnson speak.

"What's wrong Dad?" I wondered as he held me up to get a glimpse near the podium.

"I don't like this"—Dad replied. "Johnson is talking war."

"War?"

"Yes—war in Vietnam," Dad whispered to me. At nine years old, it sounded ominous.

Howling in the Afternoon

Back at home on Center Street, Mom was a great homemaker, and worked part-time as a school librarian. She encouraged my writing and my piano lessons with church pianist and organist, Ruby Pappas. The Pappas family was musical, and I loved hanging out at their home. After hearing the Beatles on the Ed Sullivan show for the first time, our dreams were to play and write music.

At Christmas, the folks gave me a long black clarinet.

Dad said, "It's called 'the licorice stick.' I love New Orleans Jazz.'"

I started playing woodwinds in the school band, but Mom discouraged my clarinet playing after hearing our Boston terrier, 'Stardust,' howl after every note.

"She is just singing along," I explained. I was told to practice in the bathroom after numerous family complaints. *I like the piano and guitar better anyway*, I realized.

Howling on the clarinet with dog Stardust

13

Our Home on Fire

While my brother, Dan, was a great example, he wasn't perfect either. As teenagers, Dan and his friends had a *Playboy Club*, located in a secret room under our home.

"Just keep your mouth shut," one older boy said. Dirty magazines were everywhere.

"If anyone asks, it's our, 'science club,'" Dan said.

Then while trading baseball cards one afternoon, Paul Pappas noticed smoke was billowing from under our home. When I raced downstairs, Dan was dousing the large flames with a hose from the backyard. A Bunsen burner had been left on during a science project.

"I extinguished the flames already," Dan said.

"Mom already called the fire department," I yelled.

Suddenly, several firefighters came running under the home. Even though the fire was already out, the firefighters started chopping away with axes at the wood.

The fire chief pulled us aside and gave us a lecture, but promised to keep the girly magazines a secret. Later, Dad discovered some of the smoldering centerfolds. The secret club was officially closed, and our Saturdays would be devoted to rebuilding the basement. Dad gave us lessons in carpentry. There were lessons in human anatomy and respect.

That week Dad gave us a stack of *National Geographic* magazines with naked African women. "Maybe you will learn something from *these* magazines, sons."

My brother would soon have his own basement bedroom. I would have new living arrangements too.

Sister Christine is Born

One night at dinner, Mom and Dad had a big surprise for everyone, "We're going to have another baby!" Dad said.

Mom wanted peace and quiet while she was pregnant. Instead of playing loudly with friends at my house after school, I started reading novels by Steinbeck and Jack London.

In the fall of 1965, my sister Christine was born at Kaiser Hospital in Walnut Creek. It was amazing to see her shock of red hair and little toes and fingers. Now there were four kids.

After baby sister Chris came home from the hospital, Mom came down with phlebitis; inflammation of a vein caused by a blood-clot. Mom went right back to the hospital and the baby stayed at home with us.

One night Dad came into the nursery as I was rocking the baby. Always the progressive psychologist, Dad came up with a new parenting idea: "I've taken too much time off work," he said. "How would you like to take a few weeks off school to watch the baby?

"Sure!" I jumped at the chance to stay home from school. Later, Christine was wheeled right into my room, "Here's your precious cargo," Dad said, heading to work.

After a couple weeks of midnight feedings and changing diapers, Mom came home from the hospital. I was glad to have her back home and a bit relieved. *Being a Mom is hard*, I thought. Then I gave my own Mom some advice: "Don't forget to burp my baby."

A Summer in Minnesota

The following summer, the folks sent me to stay with my Grandma, Francis Soldahl, in Minnesota. I would be flying to Minneapolis alone at age twelve. My parent's motto for us kids was: "responsible - independence."

Grandma was quite an entrepreneur in real estate. She owned and managed several rentals they had purchased after the Wall Street crash and subsequent depression of 1929.

I felt sorry for Grandma being a widow. 'Gram' told me Grandpa Soldahl had a heart-attack, after burying his best friend in subzero weather.

"It had taken all day to dig the grave in a blizzard," Grandma said, "when we turned up the heater in the car afterward, he just collapsed."

As a landlord, I remember the compassion Gram showed one tenant who did not have the rent money, "Pay me next week, my dear," she said.

We played her grand piano and gardened at the large green Tudor home she owned on Harriet Street. The humid evenings were spent watching the Minnesota Twins or classic films on TV.

A few days later we met up with my piano teacher, Ruby, and son Paul Pappas, my best pal from home. They were also visiting relatives in the twin cities!

Paul and I went to stay for the week, with his Grandpa in Duluth. We would be helping at his Greek style market near Lake Superior. The owner's quarters were above: "All the 7-Up you can drink is your pay," he said, "No coke!" We learned that if we did not work, we would not eat. It was in the Bible, Grandpa Pappas said.

In Fergus Falls a few days later, Uncle Fred and Aunt Mary took me golfing for the first time.

"Maybe I can play better left-handed," I said. That Saturday my uncle found a set of 'lefty' clubs at a garage sale.

"Mow the lawn in trade for the clubs," Uncle Fred offered. Cousin Sue encouraged me to practice piano. She was an accomplished church organist. That summer I would become hooked on travel, piano, golf, popcorn and old movies.

Getting ready to return home to California, I could not find my plane ticket. *Oh no!* I had left it on the plane coming to Minnesota. Calling home to apologize, my parents understood.

"Everyone makes mistakes," Dad said.

To Holden Village

As summer faded, we headed to Holden Village in Lake Chelan, Washington State; a family church camp nestled deep in the Cascade Mountains. After a twenty mile boat ride down the longest lake in America, we were staying in a European style chalet. There was hiking, arts & crafts and singing vespers in the chapel every evening.

I worked that week in the two-lane bowling alley and snack bar. Next door there was a music style nightclub for the youth called *The Cave*. It had been carved right out of an old mining cave. Half way up the sheer rock wall was a piano hoisted in place. That Friday, I climbed the tall ladder to the piano and gave my first impromptu concert. People sang along to the Beatles, *All you need is Love and Yellow Submarine*.

"Do a Gospel song," somebody called out.

Uh oh, I don't know any of those, I thought. *And this is a Church Camp.*

Then my brother saved the day, "Do *I'm a Believer*, by *The Monkees*," he said, "that one works."

On my last day there I read a framed letter on the wall. The entire camp had been purchased for one dollar from a mining company. "Everything is possible with God," it said.

Caddying for 'Chuck'

As a fresh teen, there was work at the Willow Park Golf Course back in Castro Valley. My first real job. At the Celebrity Pro/Am tournament, I caddied for the *Peanuts* cartoonist Charles Shultz.

"Call me Chuck," he said.

"My little sister has a stuffed Snoopy," I mentioned. His famous cartoon character was, *Charlie Brown*, patterned after his own upbringing.

We hit it off when I told him I was from Minnesota – also his home state. He was a true gentleman and honest golfer who loved Jazz music.

"My favorite thing is playing the piano," I said, "We saw Dave Brubeck at Cal State."

"Brubeck is a jazz piano master," Chuck replied.

"Hope you *Take Five* on this hole," I said, referring to the famous Brubeck song: *Take Five.*

"Thanks—this is only a par three hole, Shultz smiled; "Maybe you have a future in show biz…"

Charles Shultz shook my hand at the end of the round—inconspicuously handing me a folded bill.

"Wow! The guy that invented *Charlie Brown* gave me a fifty dollar tip," I bragged to the other caddies.

In those days, the government was not involved in labor laws to stop teens who wanted to work. I would be exploring many entrepreneurial jobs.

Charities and Confirmation

My folks instilled in us a sense of caring for others. One of the charitable organizations Dad helped start was called "Project Fair Chance." It was funded through a State University Grant with the goal to get single mothers off the welfare rolls and back to school, or into job training. Driving through Oakland, we often stopped at the Fair Chance offices to help out. It made me realize how fortunate we were to have an intact family.

My parents also made sure we had a faithful up-bringing. While in the eighth grade, Pastor Jensen asked me to host a talent show at our church.

"You're quite good at discovering other people's talents," Pastor Jensen said. I took it to heart.

Our confirmation service took place at Faith Lutheran Church on Redwood Road. We would be singing and reciting a scripture verse. I had not memorized mine very well.

Right before walking down the center church aisle in our white robes, I asked the guy standing by me to, "Swap Bible verses." I offered him a snickers bar for enticement. "Besides, it's my favorite one," I mentioned.

I already knew his verse, John 3:16: *"For God so loved the world, He gave His only begotten Son…,that whosoever believes in Him, shall not perish but have everlasting life."*

Church Confirmation with my family and 'Gram'

My Humbling No-Hitter

As a left-handed pitcher, my coach helped me develop a mean curveball; I was selected to play in a few all-star games. There was one season that our baseball team made it all the way to the Championship game in our Western League. Our coach, Gordon Brown had played ball for the Chicago Cubs and was everyone's favorite, *Hometown Hero*.

During the big game, it was the last inning with both teams scoreless. The other team had not reached base all afternoon.

After I struck out the next two batters, the smallest player in the league came to bat and squatted like a duck over the plate. I threw three balls and no strikes. My teammates began yelling from behind me, "Ducky-ducky! Hit him! Hit him!" We had been taunting the other team all day.

Coach Brown walked to the mound, "Do what you have to do," he said—"knock him back, Eric."

On the following pitch, I threw a fastball high and inside. It struck the batter right on the top of the helmet and he fell to the ground.

"You 'beaned him' on purpose!" a player yelled from the dugout, waving a bat at me.

The batter dusted himself off, and walked to first base. He quickly stole second base and then took off running for third to beat the catcher's throw. Sliding into base the umpire called, *"Safe!"* Coach came out to protest the call and my teammates started yelling at the umpire. Then parents started

21

booing. I looked into the stands and my Dad simply shook his head.

Frazzled, I threw the next pitch into the dirt; and the ducky runner on third base started to steal home. My dirtball pitch sailed right past the catcher and the runner crossed home plate. The 'smallest player' I had hit with a pitch, scored the winning run. Their team won the championship.

The following day, there was a newspaper article on the front of the sports page with my photo:

"*SOLDAHL* pitches a *NO HITTER* but *LOSES GAME*" Another photo showed the small batter, I had hit, hoisted atop his teammate's shoulders, as they carried him off the field triumphantly. After the game, our coach apologized to our team, "If we had won with bad sportsmanship there would be no victory." Then it was my turn to apologize...

A "No Hitter" but no "Hometown Hero"

22

The Year 1968 Changes Everything

One April day, Dad picked me up from Boy Scouts and said he had a surprise for me. My brother had a new job as the assistant manager at the new McDonald's drive-in. At the drive-through, Dad reached for our order from my brother, through the car window.

Then a news flash came over the car radio: "Dr. Martin Luther King, the apostle of non-violence in the civil rights movement, has been shot to death in Memphis Tennessee."

As I sat in the car, my stomach churned. The *I Have a Dream* speech was fresh in my memory.

"This is tragic news," Dad said, choking back tears; "Dr. King was a Baptist Minister trying to stop prejudice."

Later, on the TV news, Robert Kennedy, said, "Martin Luther King reminded us, 'Not to drink from the cup of hatred and bitterness, but one of love.'"

Campaigning for Brother Bobby

The year 1968 found me campaigning for Robert Kennedy, as he ran for President of the United States.

"He's for civil rights and against killing babies," I said, trying to sound politically astute.

So, at thirteen, I walked into the RFK campaign headquarters. They gave me hundreds of buttons, bumper sticker and posters. My own neighborhood became my "territory." In the evenings, I took walks down Center Street putting bumper stickers on every car—*without asking.*

23

The night of the Democratic primary, Bobby Kennedy was leading. A win in California might give him enough electoral votes to be the party candidate for President. I stayed up late in my bedroom to watch the election returns on a little black and white television, I bought with my paper route money.

Then; *Victory—Kennedy won!* RFK gave a speech of thanks to his campaigners and California voters. *Maybe I helped him win.* I thought, and dozed off to sleep with the TV on.

I was jarred awake by gunshots. *No!* Bobby Kennedy had been shot in the head at the Ambassador Hotel. I watched in horror as Rosie Grier, the L.A. Rams football star, wrestled with the gunman. Another Kennedy had been shot; *first the older brother and now the younger one.* Bobby lay mortally wounded on the kitchen floor of the hotel. The reporter stated Kennedy's son, David, was watching on live TV, like me, all alone in a Los Angeles hotel room.

Why are people so screwed up? I wondered, crying myself back to sleep. After Nixon was elected later that year, I considered that politics might not be the answer to the world's problems.

But my family remained very involved with political causes. That fall, Dad would speak at our Faith Lutheran Church, telling of trials while in the foxholes during World War II; "There are some 'Just Wars,'" Dad said, "we had to get rid of Hitler. But this undeclared war now in Vietnam is not a 'Just War.' Old men are using our young boys for economic gain." Dad paused, "I'm sure we can all agree on this—*All* war is hell."

Van Europe

The year I turned fourteen, the folks had another big surprise for our family.

"We're planning to take a year off and travel around Europe in a Volkswagen Camper," Dad said.

That fall, we were on a charter flight with a group of students to Stockholm, Sweden. After landing, we picked up the VW Van in Germany and traveled to our ancestral home in "Soldal Norway." The relatives there were farmers who welcomed us as long-lost kin.

We spoke little Norwegian and they spoke no English. While touring the farmhouse basement, we saw a tool chest built and signed by my Great Grandfather, Thorsen Neilson Soldahl. He had taken another similar wooden chest, filled with personal belongings, through Ellis Island when immigrating to the United States.

In Oslo Norway, my sister Nan became homesick. Her fiancé, Steve, had written her beautiful love letters and romanced her home. In a flash, she was on a flight back to the United States. She was soon married in the family home.

In France, we started traveling with two other families from the United States. They were "educators on sabbatical," and had VW Vans like us.

My brother and I grew our hair long and we grew up fast as the *Dawn of Aquarius*, approached. Hippies were everywhere throughout Europe in 1969.

"Move your Men"

After touring nearly every museum and cathedral in Paris, we visited Normandy Beach in France, and German concentration camps; Auschwitz and Dachau, in ruins. As a WWII Veteran, it was a healing return for Dad, coming to terms with the war.

Dad explained that liberating the Jews from concentration camps was justified; "At the end of the war, the walking dead came out of those camps for miles." Then he pointed to the ravaged buildings.

Later, by candlelight in the camper, Dad recalled a time in the Army while on the front lines at the Battle of the Bulge, when his Sergeant did not return from a reconnaissance mission. His 'Sarge' had been killed. As a corporal, Dad then became the highest ranking officer in his patrol.

German tanks were advancing. In the middle-of-the night, rain began pouring into the foxholes and Dad awoke to a powerful voice that told him, **"Move your men."**

Looking around, Dad noticed no one else had stirred. A few minutes later, he heard the voice more powerfully, and this time it was even clearer: ***"Move your men now!"***

As a faithful man, Dad said he *knew* the Lord had spoken these words to him. Immediately, he woke up the patrol of a dozen men and told them they needed to break camp and move to a safer position quickly. He remembered spotting a nearby cement bridge with shelter below.

Then a large man in the patrol said, "Don't listen to that guy," and went back to sleep.

Dad roused the sleeping man once again. The big man challenged Dad, who was only eighteen at the time.

"By what authority?" the man arose standing face to face.

"By the *HIGHEST* authority," my Dad stated. "The orders are to: **'Move your men now!'**"

Quickly, the men fell into line. They gathered equipment, arms and ammunition; and scurried through mud and pouring rain to the cement underpass nearby.

Right after the G.I.'s reached their new fortified position, the German tanks and mortar guns began unleashing a barrage of rounds at their empty foxholes. My father and his crew were saved! Dad gave all the glory and credit to God.

Throughout life Dad would often say, "There are no atheists in foxholes."

Camping with a VW Van for a year in Europe

Forgiveness from War

In the fall, we followed the Reine River to Munich and the Octoberfest. Tired of the VW camper bus, we stayed at the home of another psychology professor in Freiberg, Germany. I was happy to be sleeping in a real bed. One evening I noticed the German professor and my Dad were outside on a large deck overlooking the Dreisam River.

Our host spoke in a heavy German accent, "I was in the Battle of the Bulge myself," he said, "at fourteen years old." He had been with the Nazi reinforcements facing Dad, during world war two. "We were simply young boys from the German youth camps."

There was a long silence. The two men stared intently at each other, as tears welled up in their eyes. Then in the ultimate act of forgiveness, they embraced.

The Real Nails

While touring the large cathedrals of France, Spain and Italy, I noticed a discrepancy. Everywhere we went, it seemed the Catholic Church claimed to have "The Real Nails of Christ," or the "Original Crown of Thorns," placed upon Jesus' head during His crucifixion. We were charged a fee, or required to give a donation, to see these religious artifacts.

"Wait a minute," I said to one priestly tour guide; "We saw the nails of the cross in Venice. We just saw them in Madrid too... I thought there were just three nails and only one crown of thorns..."

The answers from the guides and priests were always the same, "These are the authentic ones."

Later, I questioned my parents, "Was all this about money?"

"Martin Luther had similar issues with the church over money," Dad said, "no one buys their way into heaven."

The Seas get Rough

We spent Christmas in Morocco, Africa on a hot desert beach. After New Year's, we returned through the Strait of Gibraltar on a cruise boat to the Greek Isles. One night as the waves crashed over the bow, I met a pretty girl from Crete, who grabbed my hand and led me on deck.

"Come! Everybody's dancing," she said.

Surrounding the ship's pool was a large group of folk dancers with arms linked. My brother was there and keeping step with the ethnic frolickers. Then my dance partner passed me a bottle of clear liquid. With the boat swaying in the waves, it was hard to stand, much less drink or dance.

"It tastes like licorice," I said, spitting some up.

"Don't waste it!" she grabbed the bottle from me.

"It's called, *Ouzo*," an older man laughed. Potent and fiery, it was not a drink for the faint of heart— much less a fifteen-year-old. Suddenly, the ship rocked sideways and many of the dancers started falling into the empty pool. Running to the poolside, I was relieved to see a net catching people. As we helped extract people from the pool, others ran to the side of the boat retching.

"Look!—they're sea sick," the dancing girl said.

"And drunk," a man in a white uniform scowled.

"Let's not upset Mom and Dad with this," Dan said, retrieving me from the arms of my new friend.

The Greek the Watch and the Kid

In Athens, Greece, Dan and I stayed in a youth hostel for a week. Once again it was a nice break from sleeping in the crowded camper van, with our family of five.

One night Dan was busy playing Ping-Pong with a group of Italians. Sensing an opening, I stole away undetected into the damp Aegean evening alone.

Turning a corner, a man approached me and wanted to know if I was from America.

"Please help me sell a watch to feed my family," he said with a heavy Greek accent, "Say you are out of money and need to get home."

Ever so gullible, I walked right into a clothing store to sell the Omega watch. Success! I sold it for three hundred drachmas, – about ten bucks.

After handing over the money, the older man pressed in close, revealing a gold-cap-tooth and several more watches under his coat sleeve.

"You sell more watches and you make some money," he said. When I tried to decline, he cajoled me for, *"One more watch."*

So I entered a flower shop next door. After giving my sales pitch to an older Greek lady, she burst into tears. Grabbing my arm forcefully, she pointed at a dead body lying in a coffin. They were holding a wake! It was a young man about my age. I turned for the door and an older man now grabbed my arm.

"Hold on there," he said, "I'm an American."

The man steered me quickly into the muddy street.

"I heard your story about needing a plane ticket back to the States," he said, "I'm with the American Consulate." In the dark, his white hair lit the way.

With a fast pace, we headed around the corner to the gates of the United States Embassy. My American guide waived off the Greek watch salesmen, with a few terse words.

Arriving at the Embassy, there were protestors at the large gates. "Communists," the tall American man said with disdain.

Inside the compound, we were met by several men in military uniform. Quickly, the white haired man interviewed me and determined that I was in Greece with my family; I told him they had my passport.

"So you were selling these watches for the money home?" he asked, "they're Timex watches in old Omega cases—just junk."

Placing his arms on my shoulders, the Diplomat sat me down and looked at me intently, "The young man in the coffin was a Greek student killed in Chicago just last week."

I had walked into the flower shop at the worst possible time. Ouch…

Then the Diplomat was called away unexpectedly, "Hold on a moment, kid—I'll be right back."

He has not even asked my name, I thought. Looking up at the military guard keeping watch, I asked to use the restroom.

"It's across the hallway," he nodded.

Once in the bathroom, I spotted a small open window. I jumped up on the sink and squeezed through the small opening and dropped eight feet to the soft wet ground below. I was out of the building, but still inside the gates of the large compound. The rain was coming down in sheets now. With the protestors disbursing, the guards were preoccupied. *They are not looking for anyone to escape the Embassy this troubling night,* I thought. Crouching under a large bush near the entrance, I easily slipped past the guard out the gate. A protestor was leaving with a sign and umbrella; I stayed close and found my freedom. *"Free at last, Free at last,"* I smiled to myself.

Rounding the corner, I ducked safely into a Clint Eastwood movie with English subtitles. In the dark, I laughed nervously along with the Greek crowd.

Later that night, at the Athens Youth Hostel, I was hesitant to mention my crazy sounding watch story to my brother.

"I just saw a movie in Greek with subtitles," I told Dan. "Oh, and I was interrogated at the American Embassy."

"Well, I'm glad you were not drugged," he said.

The next day we met our folks at the Parthenon. Dad walked up to us showing off his new watch.

"Ten bucks!" he said, "An Omega for only ten bucks!"

At the end of our time in Europe, we heard about huge music festivals like Woodstock back in the States. I missed my musical friends and Dan was heading to Switzerland for an immersion program in German.

"We have a plane ticket for your flight home," my folks said, "You need to make up classes with summer school." *I've been getting into trouble here too*, I thought.

My folks planned to ship the camper to the States and drive it across the country with a stop in Minnesota.

Home to America

Returning home alone that summer of 1969, I lived with my brother-in-law's folks, the Hertzog's, while making up for lost school time. Summer school at Castro Valley High was boring algebra and physics in a stifling classroom. "In Europe, I read Kafka and Kierkegaard," I said, trying to impress my school counselor.

My brother-in-law's parents were engaging as summer hosts. Will Hertzog, was a CPA and conservative politically, while Trudy a newspaper gal, "once interviewed the Beatles."

The late sixties and early seventies was a time when many disillusioned hippies and drop-outs turned away from drugs and looked to God for answers. The Jesus Movement was in full swing. There were big revivals overlooking the ocean and concerts at Golden Gate Park. My sister, Nan, and her new husband, Steve, drove us to Berkeley for church meetings and rallies. With Paul and our friend, Dennis, we entered the Battle of the Bands and were selected to open the show at Chabot College. We sang a Christian song that Dennis wrote, in a waltz tempo. It was my first real concert and we didn't get booed off stage. Girls started calling me.

A week later, I was invited to a church youth group for Movie Night. During the film, a pretty girl sitting next to me grabbed my hand and I misread her cue. Leaning over to kiss her, she briskly pushed me away.

Afterward, the youth pastor pulled me aside, "What were you thinking, Eric?" he said, "Did you think you could *make out with Marsha* while watching the Ten Commandments?"

34

Feeling disillusioned, I started hanging around with the *anti-establishment* and our new friends gave us *recreational drugs*. My band switched gears to harder rock.

One weekend, I joined a group of pot-smoking hippies at a cabin in the mountains. In the middle of the night, an older college-age gal woke me up and led me into a bedroom. Our fooling around went *way too far*. I felt conflicted the next day.

Back at home I told my brother what had happened. "At least we don't drink like our parents," I said, "those church ladies come over and have wild rum cake parties!"

One saving grace for me was Grandma, who had bought a little trailer at a park on Castro Valley Boulevard. She wanted to escape the harsh Minnesota winters. Gram had wisdom and one-liners:

"They call me a snowbird around here," Grandma joked. "Just remember—everything in moderation, Eric." When her neighbors gossiped, Gram replied, "Loose lips sink ships, you know."

Visiting Grandma's trailer was a safety valve for me. Her little place was filled with memories of Scandinavia. There were fresh baked Swedish cookies and honest conversation. We discussed politics, music and God. Every evening before bed, Grandma Frances would drink a *thimble full* of wine and say her prayers. Then she would turn on a talk radio program to keep her company throughout the night.

Late that spring, we gave Grandma a going away party. "You're Grandma needs some medical tests," Dad said, sounding a little worried.

"Maybe you can fly to visit me again," she said tearfully, before boarding the plane back to Minneapolis.

A Fateful Call

Later that month, my folks left suddenly for Minnesota, with younger sister, Christine. Grandma Soldahl was in the hospital with cancer of the esophagus. Dan and I were left home alone with instructions: "No parties—this is a difficult time—pray for your Grandma while we are away."

Two mornings later, I awoke early to the phone ringing. It was hard to hear the faint voice on the other line, but it sounded like my Grandma.

"Hi Grandma," I said, trying to wake up and sound cheerful. "How are you doing?"

Through the static, Gram sounded ecstatic, "There is nothing to worry about—it's so beautiful. Letting you know I love you," her voice faded away.

"I love you too Grandma." The phone went dead.

Then my brother came out of his bedroom, "Who was that on the phone this early?" he asked.

"Grandma…"

Dan hesitated. Half asleep, he spoke slowly, "Grandma died last night, Eric. Dad called from Minnesota, right after you went to bed—it was way after midnight."

"But I just talked to her…"

"Maybe you were dreaming," he nodded, heading back to bed; "I'm sorry to give you the sad news."

"It's all right," I said through my teenage tears.

As he walked away, Dan muttered, "Well the phone ringing did wake me up…"

Later, Nan, heard about the phone call and said, "I believe Gram was on her way to Heaven and wanted to say goodbye—she was especially close to you, Eric."

There would be some tough days ahead without Grandma around. I quickly forgot her admonition of moderation.

High School Pride

I settled into a liberal high school education during the height of an era filled with promiscuity and drugs. Our rock band played for high school dances and later for several colleges and nightclubs around the Bay.

Our Jazz band from Canyon High School would compete in Reno at the Pioneer Theatre taking first place in our division. We performed a modern *Theme to 2001* and the *Pussy Wiggle Stomp*, by Don Ellis.

One night our band director took us to a San Francisco club to hear Stan Kenton. Later, there was an empty pitcher of beer on the table and we wondered if it was safe to ride home with our soused director. My high school sports coach 'Sarge' had more conservative values.

One afternoon in the locker room 'Sarge,' grabbed me, "Cut your hair if you expect to pitch, he bellowed" The following week before a game, I stuffed my long hair into the cap.

In my second inning on the mound, I whirled around to pick a runner off second base, and my hat went flying, revealing my shock of long hair.

"Soldahl!" the coach yelled, "you're out...out of the game!" *I'm still not cutting my hair*, I thought.

After the game, our military-minded coach had me run ten laps around the track. "I'm signing you up for the cross-country team," he said, "we made State last year." Long distance running would give me time to decompress.

Longhair High School Days with Mom & Dan

A Foot in Two Worlds

Occasionally, some of the church going gals at Canyon High invited a few of us guys to sit with them on the school steps, during the lunchtime bible study.

"Let's have a sing-along," the girls would say. Sometimes I played the flute or sang: *We are one in the Spirit, we are one in the Lord*, using my old guitar brought home from Spain.

It was the beginning of my being torn between two worlds. Rock & roll friends hanging out in the school bookstore asked aloud, "Are you turning into a Jesus freak?"

My guitarist friend, Jon Robertson, defended me saying, "Eric knows what he's doing—hanging out with some of the cutest girls on campus."

One day, Skip Mesquite, a sax and flute player from the local recording group, *Tower of Power*, came and sat by me on the school steps. At the time, the band had a hit on the radio featuring his flute on the song: *Your diamonds sparkling in the Sand.* Skip was an Alumni from Canyon High and had liked my older sister. Taking the flute from my hands, he began to show me some amazing flute tricks.

Skip said, "Don't ever let anyone stop you from your dreams—saying 'you're not good enough.'"

Then the Bible group at school took turns telling about their faith. When I started to leave, one gal grabbed my arm, "Eric?" she asked in front of everyone, "It's your turn."

"Jesus is Just Alright with me," I told the group smugly, quoting a Doobie Brothers song on the radio. Right then I was 'saved by the bell' and dashed off to Jazz Band.

My parents often hosted traveling missionaries. Singers Barb and Dave Anderson came to perform concerts at our church and stayed with us a few times. Dave was a piano guy.

"Playing and singing at the same time becomes like breathing," he coached, "do it faithfully."

One day Mom called downstairs, "come quick, Barb and Dave are on Oprah," she said.

On the show, the singers gave a personal testimony about being in a plane accident while on their way to Russia. Their plane lost both engines and fell over three thousand feet into the icy Bearing Sea. Without life-jackets or rafts, they hung on to empty gas cans. Life expectancy while floating in the ocean off Alaska is for not more than fifteen minutes; it was about an hour before being rescued by helicopter. God had saved them, they said. Singing songs like *Amazing Grace,* while floating in the freezing waters helped keep them alive.

How cool to be a Musical Missionary, I thought.

Billy Graham Crusade Comes to Town

Over that summer of 1971, Jackie from the Canyon High Bible group called and was getting a group together to attend The Billy Graham Crusade.

"It's coming to the Oakland Coliseum in a week," she said excitedly.

"Count me in," I said—surprised a popular cheerleader had phoned me. That week, I was a little embarrassed to tell the others in our rock band that I was planning to attend.

During the crusade, we sat high in the bleachers. The music was beautiful and the message from the Evangelist, Graham, was even more captivating:

"Are you ready for Jesus if He came back tonight?"

The Evangelist's voice echoed over the coliseum loudspeakers, "Jesus may have had long hair, but he was no 'drop-out' and no 'cop-out,'" Graham said convincingly.

"Wow, I thought, *I've got long hair now and it's cool with Billy Graham.*

Graham continued talking about everyone being equal in God's eyes. He was openly promoting civil rights here in Oakland. My family campaigned against prejudice.

"Christ belongs to *ALL* people," Graham continued, "He's for the *WHOLE WIDE WORLD!*"

When the crowd of thousands was invited to come forward and accept Christ, as their personal savior, I thought, *It's a little too crowded down there.* Besides, had I not already been baptized as a baby? Wasn't I confirmed in Church a few years earlier at the age of thirteen?—so I sat in my chair as the others went forward to the musical strains of George Beverly Shea singing, *"Just as I am without one plea, but that Thy blood was shed for me…"*

A Poem from the Bedroom

With fall came more than a change of seasons. There was a change of heart. In the middle of the night I woke up abruptly in my basement room at Center Street. I heard "Awake!" and the sound of a trumpet on perfect pitch. Often there was music in my dreams. Opening my eyes all was quiet and dark. I felt an amazing warm glow all around me.

I recalled the night at the Billy Graham Crusade. I considered my faith and how I was conflicted—afraid to tell others about Jesus.

Why was I so reluctant to go forward in that sea of souls?

My faith had been challenged since returning from Europe and questioning the Catholic Church having so much money. The Vatican even had its own bank and currency.

My summer had been filled with parties, pot, music and girls. Now here in my room, I lit a candle and got down on my knees. I began to weep and said a simple prayer: *"Oh God, thank you for my life, please forgive me and let Jesus rule my heart from now on."* I was sixteen years old on a warm fall night in 1971.

In the morning, I woke up late for school and grabbed a doughnut while running out the door. I jogged past Cull Canyon Lake and up the hill to Canyon High. *Oh no!* Upon arriving, I remembered my poetry final was due that morning; a reading of an original poem in front of our class. While waiting in line for our teacher, Doug Rogers, I hastily scribbled something on the doughnut napkin. Of course my turn came first. This is what I read to my High School poetry class:

It wasn't when I was a baby
as water was poured from a shell upon my head
It wasn't while dressed up
as a "wise man" during a Christmas play
It wasn't while reciting a verse to a congregation
to confirm my faithful memory
And it wasn't while raising my hands shouting "Glory!"
along with thousands in a sea of new faith…
but that's o.k. if it is
But it was just last night
And it was in my little room
That an angel sang to me: *"Awake!"*
And I fell down to my knees
Thanking God for saving me--
In one word: It's spelled: "J-E-S-U-S."

The classroom was silent. I sat down and folded the napkin, and pressed it into my pocket.

At the end of class, Mr. Rogers asked for our written poems to be turned into him. I just sat there for a while contemplating my napkin. After waiting for everyone to leave, I approached his desk.

"Did you write that on your way to school?" He asked. I pulled the crumpled napkin out and nodded a 'yes' while handing it to him.

"Quite an accomplishment," he smiled, "how did you fit all that on here?" My favorite teacher held up the napkin, while a few doughnut crumbs fell to the floor.

"More importantly," Mr. Rogers continued, "You made me believe this happened to you last night."

As I backed out the classroom door, I stammered: "It did...it did."

Our Family Grows again Overnight

One day, Dad had big news after speaking out about the Vietnam War at Church.

An older Pastor said, "Maybe you can put your money where your mouth is, Tom, and adopt a family from Vietnam."

We would not be mailing a check off to some nameless family charity. A week later, the "Bui" family came to live with us. There were six of them. Our family had hosted missionaries and individual foreign exchange students before, but taking on a larger foreign family was new.

Everyone took turns cooking, doing dishes or laundry. Dinner was at two tables every evening.

"It's like a restaurant," my younger sister, Christine, said.

I was proud of our new Vietnamese family and the eldest son, Khoi, became like a brother to me. Khoi was excellent in Martial Arts. When he jumped into the air, his toe could touch the ceiling! Khoi became our band sound technician. He was tech savvy and learned from my brother Dan.

Late one night, Khoi and I were leaving a music job at the *Tuckett Inn*, in Hayward. A big biker-bouncer put his arm around my neck forcefully and said, "Don't ever bring that chink back in here." Khoi overheard him.

Before I could react, ninja Khoi whirled me away from the bouncer—and his foot was an inch from the bikers face. Still balancing on one leg, Khoi let him have it—with words:

"Next time I break your nose," he laughed. Khoi later told me that he was trained by the U.S. Military in Saigon.

"If we were not airlifted out to America, the Viet Cong would have killed my whole family," he said.

Graduation Day

Our small class of seniors at Canyon High would graduate the year of Roe vs. Wade and the opening of the World Trade Center; the world's tallest building. It seemed there were no restraints on things to come. The draft for the Vietnam War had ended right in January before my birthday.

"Quite a birthday present," Dad said; "Your future looks bright—I was drafted for WWII turning eighteen."

Paul Pappas and I had a bet to see whose hair would grow the longest, after not cutting it since the tenth grade. Now we both had hair reaching halfway down our back. We determined the bet was a tie, but "owed each other a dollar."

The night of our high school graduation ceremony, I strode proudly onto the stage to receive my diploma. Pointing in my direction a brash lady said, "Look at that guy with the long hair—he looks just like Jesus Christ!"

Without hesitating, I stopped and turned towards her, making the sign of the cross; "Bless you my child," I said.

That week I made plans to attend Cal State in the fall, where Dad was a professor. I would have the family home to myself, as my folks headed to Europe on another sabbatical.

Renovation Project

In June I saw an ad for a cabin in Guerneville, on the Russian River in Northern California. The home cost only five thousand dollars. I had saved half the money. I asked everyone for financing until finally, my brother's roommate at Cal Berkeley, Mark Phillips, agreed to go in halves with me. We planned to remodel the property and then sell it at the end of summer.

Shortly, I was hanging paneling and roofing the cabin. The labor was tedious but rewarding. *It's better than working at Hunts Cannery like we did last summer,*" I pondered.

In mid-July, I left for Yosemite, where our *Awesome Light Band* had a two week run at the Cedar Lodge. One clear night, we played outside for the staff on the Valley floor. Guitar gurus, Paul Pappas and Joel Anderson, soared in the midnight

45

air on dueling solos. Playing among the largest Sequoia Redwood trees in the world we were in nature's cathedral: *"Turn on that love light"* we sang, and everyone joined; *"Shine, Shine, Shine."*

Back at the cabin remodel in Guerneville, my partner complained, "You need to make up for your time-off, escaping to Yosemite," he said, "I did the plumbing already."

"You're right," I responded, "I'll stain the place and find a buyer too—that way we'll save money on the commission."

One weekend my brother helped us wire the home and install a new electrical breaker panel; "I borrowed a book on electricity from the library at Cal," he said.

Early the next morning, I awoke to a crashing sound as the home lurched. *Is this an earthquake*, I wondered. Running out on the deck, Mark and Dan were frantically trying to raise the foundation, as the entire cabin was slipping down the hill! A recent rainstorm had washed away several pillars.

"Get the jacks out of the car!" Mark yelled. Shortly the home was propped back up and new footings were in place.

That fall we sold our summer cabin project for almost three times the purchase price and split the proceeds.

"Let's buy a home in Berkeley," my friend said wisely, "it will be worth a fortune someday."

"Let's buy a sailboat with the money," I replied rather impulsively.

Stormy Seas

Rockin' & Rollin' on the High Seas

That fall, I attended Cal State Hayward to study music. The College teachers and parents we knew often said, "No one ever makes their living in music." I set out to prove them wrong.

One night our Awesome Light Band drove to open a show for the Doobie Brothers in the Santa Cruz Mountains. *It's our big break*, I thought. But our van filled with long-hair, pot smoking musicians had a hard time finding, *The Town and Country Lodge*. Arriving late we discovered the Doobies had already played. We played a short set to a lackluster crowd.

"The Doobie Brothers opened for us tonight," I joked proudly. But my bandmates thought it was no joke.

Afterward, the guys kicked me out of the group. I would not make the band my top priority. Many were close friends

47

from my youth and I took it hard. I retreated to the arms of my sweetheart, Barbie, who was still in high school.

Later, a couple of musical friends from college and I formed a new band to play evenings and Sunday afternoon at a popular club in Sausalito called, *Zack's by the Bay.* Since I was underage for working at the club, I tried growing a moustache. It was so light in color that I borrowed some black mascara from my sister, Nan, and colored in my faux mustache dark black. *The club owner will never know,* I thought.

"You look like a young Tom Selleck," a pretty dancer said late one night. The hit TV show "Magnum P.I." was popular then, with a buffed Selleck. I wore a jacket on stage, so as not to be called a "pip-squeak," with my lean physique.

During a break, I hunted down the gal that said I looked like Magnum PI, and we walked out on the patio overlooking the Bay with our cocktails. A moment later she leaned over and kissed me. The mascara on my moustache came right off on her face! My band mates had been watching nearby and started laughing. The poor gal ran to the bathroom crying.

"I'm glad the club owner did not see your 'masquerade,' our bandleader, Randy, said coyly; "We all could be fired if he found out you were underage."

Over the following months, I attended University classes and drove across the Golden Gate to Sausalito. We sang the pop hits, late into the night. College was getting more difficult with my band schedule, so I looked for easier classes.

The third semester of college I discovered they actually gave credit for 'Sailing 101.' So with a childhood pal, Ric Smith, we purchased a 30' Clipper Marine Sailboat. Ric was also attending Cal State; we had been friends since the third grade and had lived next door to each other in Castro Valley. As kids, we once built a submarine out of plywood in our backyard. My brother let us borrow his real periscope. Now we were shipping out on the real deal.

We moored the sailboat in Alameda and then Emeryville Yacht Harbor with an amazing view of The Golden Gate Bridge. I snuck aboard to live for a while when our musical group, "Windfall" was not on tour. The band was based out of Marin County.

They say if you can sail on the Bay, you can sail anywhere in the world. The wild ocean currents often churn the Bay waters to frighten even the most experienced boating captain.

Often during our "house gig" at Zack's by the Bay, in Sausalito, celebrities would stop by. Each week we hosted, "The world famous turtle races," and patrons would gamble on which turtle was fastest.

One night the comic actor, Chevy Chase said, "I'll buy you a drink and give you my favorite wet diaper if you let this fine lady play drums with you." It was Goldie Hawn—and she was *sizzling* on the drums.

"I played in the marching band," she smiled.

Later, Chevy brought a tray of gin and tonics to the stage, "What!" he complained, "No tip?"

Another time our small sailboat was moored near David Crosby's boat. Crosby, Stills & Nash became famous at the Woodstock concert. Crosby's large 74-foot schooner, Mayan, often appeared like an old wooden pirate ship, cutting through the waves.

Early one morning, as the dense fog hung a cover above the harbor, a dozen Drug Enforcement Agents packing pistols swarmed down the gangplanks and onto the boat next-door. One by one, the DEA led people off the neighboring craft. I peered out my little round window from our boat half-the-size. Through the mist, it seemed like those being arrested were walking the gangplank.

Then a loud voice bellowed, "Is there anybody in there?" Two DEA agents quickly fired questions at me.

"Those parties are *way out of my league*," I said in a daze.

One of the agents returned later and reported drugs had been flushed down the neighboring ship's toilet. They were picked up floating by my boat.

"You dodged a bullet," the officer warned me.

A Rolling Stone with Moss

That weekend I was at the Record Plant recording studio in Sausalito. Friends from the local band Tower of Power had invited our band, *Windfall*, to hear their album mixed. In another room, they were mixing the new Fleetwood Mac record, *Rumors*.

That night, while searching for a bathroom, I encountered the famous band that recorded hits like, *Sympathy for the Devil*.

For most of the night, I ended up playing pinball with Keith Richards, the guitarist in the Rolling Stones. Twice my age, he seemed so old. A man stood behind us in a business suit swearing at Keith. They were betting on our pinball game! For hours, it seemed, we were lost in our pinball duel.

When I finally lifted my head, it was unnerving. I had never witnessed such open use of drugs, sex and profanity. There was a bubbling hot tub in the middle of the recording studio filled with naked bodies!

Our game of pinball continued and somehow I won the final game. Keith had to be restrained from, "having a go at that pretty face." *Mine*. The man in the suit was *The Stones* manager who threw a fistful of bills at me and gave a pat on the back.

"You're a genuine Tommy-like pinball wizard," the manager said in a heavy English accent, referring to a popular film out at the time.

"I'm really an organ player..." I said awkwardly.

"I bet you are!" another Stone said to a room full of hearty laughs.

Van Morrison nodded at me from a corner in the room where he was hanging out with a couple of gals. *We should have been making music and recording,* I thought later...*what a waste.* I was squandering life - and another layer of naiveté was lost.

"Windfall" A Sailboat Under the Bridge

Dodging the Russians under the Gate

Back on the sailboat, in a twist of true irony, the song Satisfaction, by the Rolling Stones came over the radio. "I can't get no—no, no, no, Satisfaction," the words repeated. My life mimicked their words. In the morning, my boating buddy, Ric, met me at the dock. We escaped for 'safer harbors,' but the bay tides had other plans; pushing out towards open waters under the Golden Gate Bridge.

We had taken, Windfall, out a few times, but a thirty-foot sloop is no match for the Northern Pacific in rougher tides. Suddenly a Soviet tanker was bearing down on our small sailboat. The tanker appeared as a giant skyscraper coming toward our little craft. There was no wind in sight, and the sails hung lifeless. The Soviet Union tanker plowed forward;

"Great," I said loudly, "we're at the height of the cold war and getting sunk by the Russians…"

"Yeah, a ship doesn't have any brakes!" Ric called back.

Remembering the small Johnson Motor, I pushed on the auto starter. The motor did not kick over.

Ric jumped into the small hole, where the engine resided, pulling on the rope by hand; once…twice…the third time the engine sputtered and the handle broke off in his hand!

I looked up as the huge tanker descended upon us. So close, sailors lined up on the railing yelling in Russian; some horrified, some laughing. Time seemed suspended and a powerful plea echoed in my mind: *"Please God…Help!"*

Right then the sails filled up with wind. Grabbing the rudder, Ric swung the boom and we heaved over to the Port Side, lining up perpendicular to the tank's bow. The sailboat quickly SURFED away from the giant ship riding its wake.

That moment began a slow turning point in my life. I wanted to get grounded. Back on land, I quickly proposed to my high school sweetheart, hoping to settle down some. Rushing into things, we rented a small bungalow in Alameda. My fiancé was just seventeen, but her parents had eloped as teenagers and gave us their blessing. A new refrigerator too…

Jazz Lessons

One of my favorite College professors asked me to sit-in on piano with his Jazz group. It was hard to keep up. He was the bass player in a recording group called, *The Joy of Cooking*.

Right afterward, I was given home phone numbers for Jazz greats, Mose Allison and Herbie Hancock, by a jazz History teacher. Merle said coolly, "Call them to see who has the time for a lesson, or two. Don't forget to tell them I sent you." For a nineteen-year-old, I was truly 'jazzed.'

Brazenly, I contacted both Jazz greats for lessons. Herbie was more interested in the new electronic music at the time and asked me about synthesizers. "My brother knows programming," I said awkwardly.

Lessons with famous Mose Allison, were at a flat in Berkeley, and he showed me jazz piano voicings and "Jamming on Bartok"—he would blow smoke right in my face during a lesson and then leave the room saying, *"I'm listening—I'm always listening."*

One night Mose told me to come to the *Freight and Salvage* nightclub after he missed my lesson. During the sound check, he handed me a beer and said, "Play something." Mose walked around the room to check the sound system.

The owner came up and said, "Hey, what's the deal? You're just a kid." Mose waved him off and took my place at the piano. Then he grabbed a rickety chair next to the piano, "Sit," Mose said.

I stayed riveted in my chair that night from nine p.m. until two in the morning. That was my longest lesson, and I never looked at a piano the same way again.

"A piano is more than black and white keys," I thought, *A piano can become a Jazz Symphony.*

One day I would be changing the Mose Allison tune, *"I'm the one they call the Seventh Son"* to, *"He's the one they call the Risen Son,"* and play it in church.

Later, I had solo work playing piano, while wearing a Tuxedo at the fancy Flamingo Hilton in Santa Rosa. Suddenly, there was a commotion at the front door. A man

54

was being escorted forcefully outside by the Valet just for wearing shorts.

Then I saw the man in shorts was cartoonist Charles Shultz! "Hold on there," I told the valet, "I know him—this is the man who created Snoopy and Charlie Brown!

"Story of my life," Chuck said, "story of my life…"

The Impersonators

That summer, our *Windfall* band caught a break. The Anderson Agency booked us on a national tour. There was a catch. We would be backing up an Elvis impersonator.

"Steve Long is the best Elvis in the country and the money is right," Don Anderson said. It was hard to say "no" to Donny, who was a former Green Bay Packer and Super Bowl Champ. I had liked Steve Long, *Mr. Elvis*, after seeing him on TV.

We met the next day; "Our agent said you were singing in church now?" *He's a dead ringer for the King of Rock & Roll*, I thought.

"I quit show business after having drinking issues," Steve revealed. "But I'll do Elvis again—I need the money for my family."

In the morning, my parents sold me the Volkswagen Camper Van from Europe for three thousand dollars. At the fresh age of twenty-one, I became a musical gypsy. By fall we were in Tucson with Mary from *Peter, Paul and Mary*.

Next at the swanky Biltmore in Colorado, the manager called me: "Your guitarist is rebuilding a Volvo engine in his suite on the fourth floor of the hotel—if it's not gone in ten minutes you're all fired." We placed the engine on a bell cart and snuck it back down a service elevator.

Then in Joplin, Missouri, a tornado woke us in the middle of the night. *Are we on the train tracks?* I wondered. We spent much of the week clearing debris from homes and putting the musical theatre in shape.

That weekend, the Joplin Mayor spoke at our show, giving thanks to the first responders and community. "Let's thank this band too," he said.

Halfway through our first set, our Elvis impersonator gyrated into the crowd, while the women screamed.

"Is that your Mom?" our bassist Randy asked me. *Oh no! Elvis was sitting on my Mom's lap and singing Love Me Tender. Now he's giving her a scarf.* My parents had surprised me by coming all the way from Minneapolis after visiting family.

"We heard you on the radio," Mom said.

"Have you talked to your fiancé lately?" Dad seemed concerned.

"I've been good—whenever a girl approaches me, the guys tell them I'm engaged."

"Why don't you tell them?" Dad speculated.

Then leaving St. Louis my VW engine exploded. It cost me all the money I had earned on the tour to have it repaired.

In the morning, our agent called and said we needed to put together a "Big Floor Show." The engagement would be, "monumental."

56

That week everyone in the band became an impersonator. We already had Elvis, so Randy became Neil Diamond. Johnny was Tom Jones, and I would be…Donny Osmond?

"Do I really have to?—a teen idol?" I complained.

Arriving in Indianapolis, we performed across from the Indy 500 Raceway. It was the week of the big car racing event and drivers like A.J. Foyt, Al Unser, and Mario Andretti, were all in the audience.

Donning a "Donny Osmond wig," I slid across the showroom floor on roller skates singing: *And They Call it Puppy Love*—to the jeers from my own band.

Our agent loved it: "Andretti gave you free tickets to the race tomorrow." *How do these drivers stay up so late drinking like that?* I wondered, *right before the Indy 500.*

One Line in Hollywood

On our way back west we showcased in Vegas, and my Van broke down—again. After a long stint in Marina Del Rey, by the Pacific Ocean, our agent had a different type of job for us.

"They're filming Starsky and Hutch here this week—they want you as extras." The setting was supposed to be in Hawaii. *Cheap production*, I thought.

"Duck!—they're shooting at us," came my one big acting line. One take—I knocked over the plastic palm tree.

The road tour ended and we returned to Sausalito. The following week in August, the real Elvis died suddenly and our impersonator called me.

"I'm quitting the business," Steve said. "I want to get back in church. I want to honor the King." *Did he mean Jesus or Elvis?* I wondered.

Dizzy with Disney

In rock music, Bob Gardner from College at Cal State was playing with *Yesterday and Today* or "*Y&T*" and asked me to sit in on keyboards. We had both jammed with Eddie Money around the Bay.

After a few nights rocking on a Hammond Organ, with thundering music all around, Bob looked at me and said, "We can stick around here and go deaf, or make some steady money, playing pop music."

Our best gig was at Disneyland with Bob and Nancy Gardner, Dale Poune and drummer, Chris Ross. We would be a "house band," playing on the Tomorrow Land Terrace stage.

In a flash, we were "blasting off" from under the ground. The platform would rise every hour, on the hour, for thirty minutes in the land of Disney.

"Better be on that stage, or it leaves without you," Sonny Anderson, the Entertainment Director told us. Our first week at the Magic Kingdom, all of our hair was chopped off at the Disney barbershop. *The Beach Boys and Jan and Dean play here with long hair*, I thought. Then our first big paycheck arrived and we all agreed to the moral Disney code. The comedian and actor, Steve Martin, was a host. He had short hair too.

Keeping with the program, our band name changed from *Caught in the Act*, to *Straitlaced*.

58

"It's all part of The Act"

On our days off, I flew home to the Oakland airport preparing for our wedding. I had not seen my fiancé much over the past year.

"I commute by jet to Disneyland," I bragged to a friend.

Then, one morning my flight was running a little late. I took the monorail in from the Disneyland Hotel station, to make up for lost time. The words, *"Better be on that stage,"* echoed in my ears. I arrived just in time to grab my clothes, but the stage was rising. I jumped on at the last minute and began changing fast. A group of tourists and young school girls were watching me from the top as the stage ascended. The young teen girls started pointing and screaming at me.

When the stage broke the surface overlooking Space Mountain, I was still pulling up my tight spandex pants. Crouching behind an amplifier, I finished dressing. Standing up quickly, I became lightheaded, and fell backward.

Our lead singer, Nancy, thought fast saying, "It's all part of *The Act* folks."

After the show in the dressing room, our band had a meeting. I needed to shed the *pop star persona*, and *not my clothes*, was the consensus.

Disneyland and Harrah's Group

From Disney Fun to Fast Living

The following month we were hired at Harrah's in Lake Tahoe. Overnight we went from straight-laced Disney to an atmosphere filled with gambling, drinking and drugs. Many nights there were famous stars like Sinatra, Wayne Newton or Bill Cosby hanging around drinking and gambling.

The nicer celebrities like Sonny Bono were into hiking and skiing. One afternoon a pair of skis almost took my head off in the Harrah's Lobby. Helping me to my feet, the skier looked familiar. It was John Denver. After a quick apology, I mentioned our group played upstairs on the top floor.

"We start at the top and work our way to the bottom here," I smiled, "but we want to play our own music like you."

"I am my songs," John Denver said, "just be your songs."

60

Married at 22

That summer, I married my high school sweetheart. A Lutheran Pastor friend, Lee Sather, performed the ceremony. My new wife was not keen on attending church. She did not seem excited about having children either. I hoped marriage would change her mind.

Our band was booked for the season at Harrah's Resort and Casino in Tahoe. My wife got a job at the Forest Restaurant as a hostess there on the eighteenth floor. Our Swiss style chalet was furnished and included in our pay.

"I'm not going to gamble this summer," I told Bob Gardner, "hold onto every paycheck for me." Back in Castro Valley that fall, we bought a small condo with the money we had saved.

Watching TV with a hangover one morning, I saw a distinguished looking man speaking about, *"Getting a life—by getting a real estate license."* So I decided to forego the life on the road in music and enrolled at the Lumbleau College of Real Estate. I longed for a family with children.

"We better settle down first," my young wife said.

While studying for my real estate license, I started working for my brother, Daniel and a family friend, Charlie Babb, who was the Manager at The National Industries for the Blind, in Emeryville. I liked driving the forklift and talking to the hardworking sightless men and women.

My older co-workers, who are blind, have a much clearer view of things than I do, I realized one day.

61

Eye of the Duck

The following month there was another wedding. This time my Vietnamese friend Khoi was marrying.

"Please bring your Mom and Dad," Khoi said. His bride was a beautiful Viet gal named Kim-Loan.

At the traditional ceremony near the Bay, there were bright colors and long flowing silk gowns. We were honored to be seated at the head table by Khoi's grandfather.

"This food has a lot of tentacles," I laughed. There was a large cooked duck in the middle of our table. Peering around the room, I saw each table had their own duck in an upright position.

Finally, Grandpa used toothpicks and plucked an eye from the duck and swallowed it, "Mmmm, he said, rubbing his belly for effect. Then he plucked the other ducks eye from the socket and put it to my lips. Everyone stopped what they were doing at the wedding party and watched us; a hush fell over the room.

"It's to test your bravery and honor," Khoi smiled.

Thinking fast, I grabbed a champagne glass and hit the top of grandpa's chopsticks, knocking the duck's eye into the bubbles. I quickly gulped down the entire glass including the duck's eyeball.

My Mom rolled her *own* eyeballs in horror.

Rubbing my tummy, I said, "That was delicious."

"I don't know if that counts—but we're out of eyeballs," Khoi laughed.

A "Byte" from the Apple

Ahead of their time, my brother and Charlie Babb opened one of the very first personal computer stores. It was called the "Byte Shop" located in Walnut Creek. I picked up a couple of hours working on weekends. One day, there was a scruffy looking fella buying parts. It was Steve Wozniak, who was just forming Apple Computers with Steve Jobs. Dan took him into the back where he was building computers. Overnight, Apple became their biggest client.

"Apple wants to trade us 5000 shares of stock for computer parts," Charlie said one day. So Charlie and his dad visited the Apple assembly plant.

"They're working out of a two car garage in Los Altos," they reported, "trading parts for their company stock is *way too risky.*"

The Byte Shop hit rough times when Carter became President and gas lines circled the block. Interest rates were at 18%, and the Byte Shop had its line of credit called in by the bank. Charlie Babb advised me to concentrate on real estate and finish my college education.

When my real estate license arrived, I started selling property in my hometown of Castro Valley. After a few big commissions came in, I transferred my College credits to the University of San Francisco, for a combined program in Organizations and Management.

USF was a Jesuit University. A religious class was required to graduate. My favorite class was 'Judaism,' where we spent a week in residence with a Rabbi. We read the Torah in Hebrew, learned the Mosaic Law and cooked kosher foods. My college graduation ceremony was a lonely event when my parents were the only family in the audience.

"Where's your wife?" a fellow female graduate asked me, foretelling of trouble ahead.

Life in the Financial Fast Lane

In business, I formed a Commercial Real Estate company and hit a crest in the Bay Area real estate boom. I became a "workaholic—playaholic." The hard worker who could not wait for the country club weekend, to escape the pressures of the world, with whatever vice is around. I was coming into a time when I would have success by the standards of the world, but lose myself in it all.

We had no time for faithful things. It was easier to sleep in on Sunday mornings and watch the Forty-Niners, after a night on the town.

In relationships and business, I was self-absorbed. The book on my dresser was titled, *Looking Out for Number One*. It was hard taking a deep look at myself. Then my Dad gave me an introspective men's book, *The Man in the Mirror*. I read,

"You find yourself spending your whole life climbing the ladder of success, only to learn when you reach the top, it has been leaning on the wrong wall the whole time."

One morning, I forced myself to look in the mirror; in my eyes I saw a superficial person, without much to like.

That night, after working in the city, I found a pamphlet during "happy hour," in the restaurant bathroom. The tract showed a picture of the cross of Jesus bridging the gap between a person and God. It read: *Sometimes when a person has money or position, they do not see the need for God. They feel self-reliant.* That was me. There was plenty of money; it seemed, with all the credit cards being sent to us in the mail. I had just purchased two four-unit apartment buildings at a foreclosure auction.

"Where did you get the money?" my wife asked.

"No worries, I just walked into the bank with a few golden credit cards."

"As long as we can still go to the Caribbean next month," was her response.

"Wizard of the Keyboard"

One day there was a break from my hectic schedule. My old baseball coach, Gordon Brown, stopped by the Allied Brokers real estate office on Redwood Road. He was also the building inspector. "We want you to join our musical group at Faith," Gordon said, referring to the church where I had grown up. "We do the special events, singing Barbershop and Gospel harmonies, he explained.

My sister, Christine, was assisting me at the office over the summer and encouraged me to join them. She had sung in choir. Maybe I didn't have to give up music after all.

On the eve of our first concert, "Doc Lloyd," an old family friend, gave me a large pointy red hat and posted a sign on the piano, *Eric: Wizard of the Keyboard.* Returning to my old church for the first time in years, the sign and funny hat were embarrassing, but truthful to my state; they

65

represented my little *Scarlett Letter*. I felt conviction for my recent past. But everyone at church just showed love.

Then in the middle of a ragtime tune, I looked up to see my old piano teacher, Ruby Pappas, smiling in my direction. It felt like a homecoming for everyone, with my brother and sisters there too.

"Why doesn't your wife ever come?" Doc asked

Soldahl Siblings at Center St: Christine, me, Daniel and Nan

A Grand Tetons Family Reunion

With the arrival of summer, there was a change of scenery. The Soldahl and Smith families from Minnesota were having a big family reunion in Wyoming. We would be camping in the shadow of the Grand Teton Mountains.

"Why don't you go alone?" my wife said, "I'm busy moving offices next week.

"If you worked for me—you could come," I said.

"You can't afford me," our fights often played out. *She was right, I could not afford her.*

On the plane flight into Jackson Hole we hit an air pocket and plummeted like a stone—thousands of feet in several seconds. I was happy to be strapped in, but my drink hit the ceiling; the flight attendant hit the ceiling too! Moments later she fell to the aisle as the light aircraft found an updraft. Shaky but unscathed, passengers departed the plane in a daze.

At the campground, our Minnesota relatives were all there: *Aunt Mary, Uncle Fred, Cousin Sue, Mark and Paul;* sounding like a Paul McCartney song. Over the week we fished, hiked, and toured Yellowstone. By night there were campfire sing-a-longs, just like old times in our youth. It was truly wonderful being with the relatives, however, at night it was lonely in my cold sleeping bag. All had their own families.

The following afternoon I took a canoe ride with my older cousin, Mark. The white-capped Tetons reflected a perfect image on the water.

"Remember canoeing on the Gunflint Trail into Canada?" I said, "not much has changed with everyone."

My wiser cousin was more honest, "Marriage and children have changed my life a lot," he said, "It takes effort."

Light struck the colored stones beneath our canoe. The iridescent setting was intoxicatingly beautiful.

"I'm having trouble in my marriage," I revealed.

"Call me anytime, if you need to talk," Mark replied with empathy, handing me the oars on shore.

Unhappy High School Reunion

Arriving home on an early flight from Wyoming, my wife picked me up in a new sports car. She fired off questions in the fast pace of city traffic: "Did you forget the High School Reunion tonight?—when's the last time you had a shower?"

"Just drop me at the office," I replied.

By sunset, I was sporting a new Jerry Garcia tie and downing cocktails at the Crow Canyon Country Club. It was good to see old friends from Canyon High. Many, I had known since the third grade.

A friend told me, "Sometimes when people are drinking, they forget they are married." He was right.

My wife and I went separate directions that evening.

At one point, I spotted her embracing an older man. She pressed close to his Armani suit—lost in a slow dance; *I hate that song: "Feelings,"* I thought. Ironically, it was my old Jazz band from Cal State on the stand.

Later, I was flirting with one of our former school cheerleaders with a group of guys and my wife approached suddenly. Spinning me around, she slapped me in the face!

Did that just happen? My mind raced. *The whole school just saw that...* She turned around, grabbed her purse and left me stranded at the reunion.

The next day I confronted her, "How could you do that in front of everyone? I would never slap you or leave you like that." *The truth was I had abandoned her in our marriage.*

"Let's not talk about it anymore," was all she said.

68

By that Sunday night; I was so distraught, I ended up in the Hospital Emergency room with severe chest pains.

"Better slow down," my cardiologist cautioned, "stress can be a killer."

"How many men die from a broken heart, Doc?"

"No Problem"

With our marriage in big jeopardy, a counselor recommended, working for a couple of charities together. I was often tapped to play piano to help out at these charity events. With the "Make a Wish Foundation," we helped send a boy to Disneyland. He was ten years old but had the disease that made him look eighty.

At a Boys and Girls Club opening in Sonoma, there were names like Coppola, Montana and George Lucas dining with us under a big cheap tent. When taking place at upscale wineries, my glass was never empty. Playing Jazz piano for the celebrity donors, I would eye my glitzy wife suspiciously. Instead of making things better for our marriage, we found ourselves drinking more. Arguments would often follow.

Then as a Realtor, I sold two pastors their first homes. Asked to lead the music for a Sunday evening church service, I saw it as a great sign. Maybe my wife would come.

"I have to work," she said.

"On a Sunday night?"

That week I started golfing with the pastors. It was hard for me to be honest with my pastor pals about my poor marriage situation. Secretly, I was behind on my mortgage; a big house with even bigger payments. The money flowed in, but was spent even faster to, *Keep up with the Joneses*, next door. In my case, it was an Oakland Raider defensive end named Todd Christiansen; I had sold him the huge home by mine. Then my neighbor introduced me to Jim Plunkett, his Super Bowl quarterback. A week later, I sold my first large commercial building to a few of these famed Raiders. I was able to stall the foreclosure and eventually sell our big home.

My pastor buddies offered up positive words of encouragement—even while I was swearing at a bad golf shot. Life had more clarity when hanging around these *Holy Golf-Ball Rollers*. But I had a hard time with the truth.

"Were you really drinking and playing poker last night?" they might ask me out of concern.

"Not a problem—didn't Jesus make wine out of water?"

"Why are you moving back to a condo?"

"No problem," came my reply.

"Are you getting a divorce?" *No problem...*

One Way Street

Moving to Chico, California, brought a fresh start. My plan was to open another Commercial Brokers office and grow a diverse financial services company. My office building soon included accountants, attorneys, stock brokers and property managers.

It helped to join the Chamber and Exchange civics groups meeting weekly. The Exchange group worked to provide battered women and children housing, so I thought it was a good fit for a Realtor.

After reading *Think and Grow Rich* by Napolean Hill, I realized it was more about associating with good folks and providing them a service, rather than about the money. The town leaders started stopping by my office to chat.

Shortly, Dr. Vietti, the Dean of Business at the University, set me up with one of the world's first Internship Programs. Our firm grew overnight with bright young minds.

One day an older man called and wanted to sell his run-down motel on The Esplanade, "I'm dying of cancer," he said.

After dropping a large set of keys on my desk, he continued: "Look—just sell the motel and send me the money in Mexico…"

Enlisting the help from our civics group and a local church, the property was purchased by a 501c3 non-profit that was formed. A few months later, several abused mothers with children were residing at the newly renovated motel; there were nice kitchenettes too. *All these kids need Dad's*, I thought.

Walk In — Dance Out

After forming several investment groups, the company expanded from apartments and office buildings into restaurants. Our signature restaurant and nightclub was *LaSalles*, "A Chico Tradition Since 1896." The first day at the restaurant I received a call.

"Hi Eric, this is Mayor Nichols, are you ready for the Governor's Luncheon tomorrow?"

"What?" I asked alarmed.

"Senator Feinstein will be coming too."

Uh oh—it turned out our restaurant was the annual site for the State's political elite. After hiring the best catering company in town, we muddled through the event.

A week later, I was chairing a committee for the Mayor on a new enterprise zone at the Airport. After that I was appointed to find land for a new events center. I started working from morning until night with parties' in-between. At the club, our musical group often performed and I booked groups like the Van Morrison band. All of our staff wore shirts that said: *Walk In and Dance Out.*

Soon, our musical group '*The Ammin' City Jammin' Band,*" was the toast of the town. The band consisted of several medical doctors. We aimed high for the biggest venues around; including concerts with the likes of Kenny Loggins and Michael McDonald. Prior to one big event, we even purchased a couple of limousines. Great fun, but I started taking it all a little too seriously.

At the end of our summer concert, Kenny Loggins and Michael McDonald motioned for us to join them on stage, in front of nearly ten thousand people, singing on the old Percy Sledge tune: *When a Man Loves a Woman.*

Here my marriage was on the rocks, but I thought, *This song will really get to her…now she won't leave me.* I was wrong. After the big show, my wife filed for divorce.

So like most men, I kept my feelings hidden. I fuelled my lonely life with liquor, work and big dreams. Now in my early thirties, I went into full-blown mid-life crisis.

Reality Show and TV Ads

That month, the Lifetime Network came to videotape our band for one of the first ever reality TV shows with, *The Dr. Rockers.* Brev Creech, a plastic surgeon, was our ringleader.

After the show aired, I was asked to portray an optometrist in a national TV commercial.

"Millions will see this," the producer said. In the advertisement, I was dressed in a white doctor smock while examining a patient. I removed their bandages and instantly replaced them with eye glasses; *Poof!* It was humbling when they dubbed in a, *more mature sounding voice*, for mine. I didn't know the difference between a suture and a scalpel but people began calling me, "Dr. Soul."

It was surreal to have strangers on the streets stop me and say, "Don't I know you?"

"I'm not a real doctor, but I play one on TV," became my favorite line. My head was filling with air. I had been neglecting my businesses, but I had a few key employees that kept things running more smoothly than I did.

"I'm better at sales and the big picture," I told my staff often heading out the door. I would often take an extended hiatus from the pressures of restaurants and real estate.

One brisk winter day, I drove with Doc Brev Creech up the Mt. Rose Highway to go skiing. I was excited to show off my "new talking car," from Japan. As we laughed along the way, the sky suddenly turned all white with snow flurries.

"White out!" Doc said, "There's a snowplow coming right for us!" As I pumped the brakes for traction, there was a powerful jolt to the car and a deafening noise. An oncoming car missed the snowplow, crashing into my driver's side. Metal was twisting around me. On impulse, I landed on Doc.

Shortly, a Mt. Rose security officer was examining us for injuries and drove us directly to the hospital in Incline Village. Thankfully, no one was hurt, but the car was totaled. A big dent went into my armor that day. Laughter had left for now.

Country Concerts

That next Spring, Disney writers and recording artists, Stratton and Christopher, called me to perform in a series of summer concerts with them. Before long, we were flying to the Calgary Stampede.

"Over one million people will hear you this week," the event manager said. It was all hard to believe.

Then we jetted off to New Orleans and a CMA, Country Music Awards event. My musical patrons, Bob and Gary, acted as the hosts. We were working with Dolly Parton and Kenny Rogers. My Uncle Fred and Aunt Mary, were living in Sun City West, near Phoenix, and surprised me at the show.

Then we had a featured spot with the Charlie Daniels Band. I had not been nervous the entire tour.

Now my Mom and Dad had called to say they would be attending the concert and meet up afterward. During our sound check, I had a funny feeling. Bob and Gary had asked Charlie Daniels to, "Give our new piano player a bad time, *Just for fun.*"

Finally, while performing for thousands of wild country fans, including my parents, Charlie came and stood right next to me wearing his ten-gallon cowboy hat and giant belt buckle. His arms were crossed and there was a big scowl on his face. He peered intently at my piano during a solo.

"Do something," I heard. The bright spotlight found us. I pulled out a couple tricks and started playing the keyboard with my right foot, *Jerry Lee Lewis style.* Charlie just shook his head. Spinning around, I began playing the piano behind my

back: *As the Thunder Rolls*. Stalwart Charlie didn't move a muscle.

After our set, the drummer, Hal Race and I were playing ping pong, at a table set up behind the stage.

"It might help you unwind," Hal said.

During the encore of the song, *The Devil went down to Georgia,* I slammed a table tennis shot so hard, I lost my balance. Falling forward on the ping pong table, it broke right in two! The song blared: *The devil went down to Georgia looking for a soul to steal…*

After finishing an encore, Charlie Daniels came right over to me. "Are you the SOB who broke my ping pong table?" he thundered.

"Let me buy you a drink," I replied feebly.

"And a new table," he glared—then smiled.

Later, after a couple of shots—not with gun bullets, Charlie chuckled, "It's not even my doggone table."

When my parents came backstage; I was a little soused, but they were a welcome sight. They always encouraged me during these trying years.

"The paperwork came through on my divorce," I told my folks, "It's final." Once again I did not take blame.

"Sorry the counseling did not help," Dad, the psychology professor empathized.

"She didn't want kids," I explained. The truth was my ex probably didn't want kids…*with me*…

Stick in the Back

The following week we were in Redding, California, at the Civic Auditorium, for another big concert. Merle Haggard, the famous Country singer, lived nearby, and I had recorded at his home studio with my mandolin friend, Steve Brown.

"I was recording at Merle's house," I boasted, "Haggard said we just missed Willie Nelson and Johnny Cash."

On our last song, we launched into *"God Bless the U.S.A."* by Lee Greenwood. Then with shouts, the crowd rose to its feet from their comfortable seats. There was screaming and more thunderous applause. *We're getting an encore here,* I thought arrogantly, taking a solo. Suddenly, a sharp jolt dropped me to my knees on stage. Hal, our drummer, had thrown a drumstick hitting me squarely in the back.

"What are you doing?" I yelled towards Hal over the music and loud crowd noise.

Hal pointed with another drumstick already in his nimble fingers—behind us—towards the back of the large stage. There was a gigantic American Flag descending slowly over us. It was *HUGE*. Fifty feet across at least. The patriotic crowd had been clapping for the flag and what it represents and not me…

I returned to my real estate offices in Chico half-heartedly, ready to escape at any time.

Stanford – Détente and the Venetian Room

My conservative client, Marshal, called early one morning, "There's an international political gathering today and you're going with me."

"I am?—It's still dark outside."

"This is a world changer, Marshal said, "It's at the Hoover Institute, on the Stanford campus." Marshal owned an agency that had access to press passes. We drove quickly to Palo Alto and by sunrise I was surrounded by famous reporters.

Previously, President Ronald Reagan had met Mikhail Gorbachev from the Soviet Union at a summit in Switzerland, to end the cold war.

"They're breaking up the Soviet Union into states," a reporter told me, "they have a 'Georgia' in Russia too."

"The Berlin Wall came down in November," I added, "Is this a policy meeting?"

"This is the public face—it's closed door for that."

"Secretary of States Kissinger and George Shultz are here," Marshal said, "It's the first time Gorbachev has visited outside of Washington."

Then after receiving a tip about a private reception, Marshal grabbed me. "Let's go!" he said. Hopping in his convertible, we were quickly winding our way through the steep streets of San Francisco.

Arriving at the Fairmont Hotel, we found the world-famous Venetian Room. They were setting up for a banquet.

This is where Tony Bennett sings, I thought in awe. Eyeing the nine-foot grand piano, something inside said, *"Play."*

Shortly, I was playing musical standards like *I Left my Heart in San Francisco*, as the Hoover Institute crowd arrived. When a hotel manager came over, Marshal spoke to him. Suddenly, the manager leaned on the piano and said, "Play something appropriate—Gorbachev is here!"

"How about 'Hail to the Chief'" I smiled, launching into the first stanza. In mid song, two men in black suits were suddenly ushering us out the back way through the kitchen.

"You don't have proper clearance," a man in black said.

"Well, so much for *friendly détente*," I laughed.

Loma Prieta Rocks the State

My next getaway was unexpected. As I turned on the TV for the World Series between the Oakland A's and the S.F. Giants, an earthquake jolted me right into the TV set. A slow long roll followed and I noticed the swimming pool was rocking back and forth, as water poured out the sides.

This is one big earthquake, I thought, *maybe centered in the Bay Area...*The answer came when the broadcast from the game in San Francisco had stopped and I could not reach family in Castro Valley.

Once again, Marshal came by the home with a challenge: "Look, both of our families are in the Bay Area," he said, "let's see if they are all right and then join the relief efforts—hundreds of people are trapped under the Nimitz freeway right now."

"Let's go—a section of the Bay Bridge collapsed too."

Arriving in the East Bay, we found our families shaken, but still in one piece. Signing on with the Red Cross, we were sent to *Ground Zero*, in Santa Cruz. The National Guard led our way into the downtown devastation. Everywhere, buildings lay in ruins. That week we dug people out and removed dangerous debris. The aftershocks were unnerving.

When I complained about wearing a hard hat, a supervisor pulled me aside, "A worker died yesterday when a brick from a chimney fell and landed on his head."

Discovering I was a Realtor, he sent me into the nearby mountains to help check on properties. Many gas leaks were starting fires. In one home I encountered a man who would not leave, even though the smell of propane was everywhere.

"Here's how you get people out," another supervisor said, handing me a large black felt pen. "You ask them for the names and numbers of their *next of kin,* then pull out the pen and tell them you need to write the information on their arms—then pause and say, 'we need to know where to send your body, if there's anything left after the house explodes.'" It sounded so callus, but on my next stop it worked!

In the end, 67 people had died, with nearly 4,000 folks seriously injured in the Loma Prieta Quake.

Back home in Chico the next week, I slipped into my old self-serving ways.

Life Down a One Way Street

Turning thirty-five was a milestone I did not want. I continued in a pattern of partying. Church was for the holidays. Every two weeks I had to make payroll and it felt

80

like a burden. At every opportunity I ran to my vacation condo in Tahoe at Northstar.

"You have forty-two employees now," my secretary told me one day, "That's a big responsibility." *I felt anything but responsible.*

One dark night, I went to lock up our *LaSalles* Restaurant and discovered the bartender was drunk. He was lying down behind the bar with the cash register drawer left open.

Leaning over the antique bar, I pointed a finger, "If you were not so wasted, I'd fire you!" Then with a *Can't beat them join them attitude*, I slammed two shots of pricey tequila and walked out the door.

On my way home, I was stopped by the Chico Police going the wrong way down a one-way street. A police car was heading right for me! Moments later, I staggered from the car. Thankfully, the officer knew our Greg Scott Band—the cop was the former sax player in the same group—*What luck*, I thought. The officer graciously delivered me home without even giving me a ticket.

"How do you know where I live?" I asked.

"I have your driver's license in my hand," he said.

The next day at our exchange club luncheon, I boasted about the incident: "Well I guess you 'can fool some of the people some of the time...'"

Another Realtor quickly admonished me, "Sometimes 'letting someone off the hook' is no help at all," he replied. "I just lost a close friend who was hit by a drunk driver."

When that lost summer ended, there was more drama.

From Hero to Zero - *Again*

One Friday evening, as autumn leaves fell across the road, I headed up Highway 50 towards Tahoe to hook up with a much younger gal I was courting.

"I want you to meet my family," means it is getting serious. Conversation often turns to marriage.

After brokering my largest Commercial Real Estate deal to date, I was riding high. It was an entire Western Coast Hotel Chain. The eighty-seven-year-old owner had met me in Denver, and we had quite a rapport. Now I was driving a red Porsche Carrera with a built-in cell phone. People would gawk just to see what a car phone looked like in 1990. So far, I had sold just one of the hotels, but was spending like the commissions had been paid on all twenty of them.

Just that week, the Enterprise Record Newspaper ran an article on me with the headline: *Is this the New Trump?* My secretary spoke two words: "ego trip"— *maybe she was right.*

Stopping to refuel in Placerville, California, at a 76 Gas Station, I was gazing down at my new snake-skin cowboy boots; *I'll make quite an impression on her family*, I thought. At that moment the car cell phone rang. It was my new heart-throb.

Speeding away from the pump as I chatted on the phone, I felt something jerk violently. Turning my head around, I saw flames shooting skyward. *I better drive fast to get out of here.* As I gunned the Porsche, I heard the awful scraping of metal. Some jerk had forgotten to disconnect the gas handle from his tank. The whole tank had been pulled over and flames were blazing. Oh, no—I realized. *The Jerk is me!* The nozzle

82

was still sticking out of my Porsche gas tank and the entire gas pump had fallen. The pump was dragging behind my car. Quickly jumping out of the Porsche, I ran to an open dirt area away from the flames and bent down staring at the ground.

"Please God help," I implored.

"Look up," I heard.

Seeing that other lives may be in danger, I ran back to the pumps at the gas station and started yelling for everyone to flee. Leaning inside my car from the passenger's side, I dialed 911 on my new car phone. Flames were now shooting twenty feet in the air, from the location where the gas dispenser once sat. I ran inside the station and the attendant handed me a large fire extinguisher.

"I am an auxiliary firefighter," he said excitedly. "This is your lucky day."

Right, I thought, feeling sick to my stomach. *My lucky day, where I blow up a gas station.* We both ran outside to the pump trying to extinguish the roaring fire. I was expecting to be engulfed in flames. We sprayed the foam everywhere. But every time we doused the pump with fire retardant, the flames would die out briefly – and then roar back to life. Fast approaching, the sirens from several fire engines were a welcome sound.

A fireman hopped off a truck and shouted over the commotion, "Did you shut off the main valve?"

The gas station attendant looked around meekly, and the fire was quickly extinguished with one turn of a large valve.

Pulling me aside later, the chief said, "You caught a break here—we issued a citation to this gas station just last week, for not installing the required 'release valve' on the pump handle. It's supposed to detach the nozzle when someone forgets to put it back."

"Thank God no one was hurt," I stammered.

Once again, I was going to be let off the hook.

A couple of days later, at Thanksgiving dinner, '*Great Grandma,* Mary,' held up a newspaper showing a picture of me standing by the burned-out gas station and the Porsche: *Some Turkey helped himself to the whole pump,* it read.

"Front page news around here," '*GG*' said with a smile. For now, I would be *the butt of a few jokes.* It felt like my life had undoubtedly gone from *"Hero to Zero,"* in record time. *Why do I turn to God ONLY when big trouble comes?* I wondered.

Done Deal

Two weeks later, I ended up losing the mega-million dollar Hotel deal. The Hotel owner's younger wife had filed an injunction, and now my biggest client was committed to a Mental Facility.

"She's having an affair with a much younger man in the company," one lawyer said. "He was running their health clubs. The old man canned him—Let it go or you're next."

Over the following week, the west coast was pummeled by one of the largest storms on record.

"When it rains it pours," my assistant, said one day giving more bad news, "the roof caved in last night at Godman Avenue."

What!? I thought, *our big apartment complex...* "Was anyone hurt?" I asked rhetorically, running out the door. Thankfully, no one was injured, but lawsuits followed, and insurance did not cover everything.

Afterward, I put my real estate office building up for sale. Even worse I had to lay off most of the staff.

Since moving to Chico, I had denied problems in relationships, in business and in facing my own addictions. Addicted to work, partying and striving for what I believed was *success*. My debts were many, but I did manage to hang onto one property. A mini-storage complex we were developing in Yuba City, I named it *Safe and Sound Self Storage.* My life was anything but, "Safe or Sound."

One day at the mini-storage office I said, "We did it! We just rented our last unit. Number three hundred."

My last remaining partner reminded me, "Don't get so cocky—we're just, 'Keepers of the junk.'"

He's right, I thought, *my life is pretty trashed too.*

A Hometown Christmas

In Chico, I married the free-spirited younger gal. She dismissed my being in the news and setting the gas station on fire. She overlooked my financial woes. We both wanted children and she enjoyed cooking.

My new wife had a Grandfather that was a Baptist preacher, "Let's go to church on Sunday," she said.

In late fall, we planned a benefit concert and Christmas show at the Laxon Auditorium with the singer, Greg Scott, and Producer, Kurt Kearnes. The three of us were known as, *The Fabulous Nicklaus Brothers.* We sang our own Christmas songs while dressed in Santa outfits.

One night we wrote an anthem, *Christmas Time in my Town.* In December, the song had radio airplay. Kurt also sent the song to the Gulf War Veterans via Armed Services media and radio. The Associated Press picked up the story nationally. Soldiers wrote home about the theme of the song and their trials of being away from home at Christmas.

That week, we were on a morning TV show and concerts followed. A large Baptist church choir joined us and opening night the powerful singing shook the large auditorium.

The Christmas Time stanza rang out:

"Let's hold on to each other and raise our voices high
Brother to brother – where angels sing on high
Let's all share the spirit, Christmas time will bring
Everyone join in now, everybody sing:
Christmas Time in my town
The most special time of year
Christmas Time in my town
Folks are filled with cheer
Christmas Time in my town
The best place that I know
Christmas Time in my town
It might even snow..."

Christmas Time in My Town, with Choir

The following Sunday found *The Fabulous Nicklaus Brothers* singing with the Baptist choir at their historic church in Chico. During the sermon, Greg Scott leaned over and whispered, "Let's donate the money from our concerts to paint the church."

Children Change Everything

On Christmas Day we found there was a baby on the way! I had always wanted children. God was blessing us.

After consulting a few wise friends from our doctor band, I planned a break from business to concentrate on music. This would free my time during the day to spend with family.

At a Calvary church the following week, Pastor Sam Allen gave a sermon on Jonah, who had run from his, "God given mission." *Maybe I have been running all these years too,* I thought, *Maybe God has a better plan for my life.*

After church, I reassured my new wife I would be there for her and the baby. The next few months seemed to fly by with doctor appointments and setting up a nursery. With

87

many of my wife's family living in the Sierras, we decided to have the baby at Barton Memorial in Tahoe.

The morning of the birth; we had stayed up all night, and the labor was intensive. It was a breach birth and my wife fought through the pain. Worried, I never left the room. Well after dawn, the baby weighed in at exactly ten pounds.

That night, I was playing music with my old Disneyland friends, Bob and Nancy Gardner, at the Harvey's Casino by Lake Tahoe. In the middle of our last set, Ringo Starr, the famous Beatle, came walking through and stopped to watch us. Ringo's son, Zack, was standing by his side. Both father and son folded their arms while holding drumsticks. They had just finished playing a large concert in the summer stadium.

Suddenly, Bob Gardner stopped our music and announced, "Our keyboard player, Eric, just had a ten-pound baby this morning."

"Boy, did it hurt," I said rubbing my belly. Then Bob surprised me passing out cigars to everyone, including Ringo.

"This is the first time playing drums with me own son, Zack," Ringo said loudly, holding up the cigar.

That night, back at the hospital, I checked on my wife who was sound asleep. "Better not wake her," a nurse said.

Then I found Grayson in the nursery. I already recognized his cry. It was four o'clock in the morning.

"Can I hold my new son," I asked the charge nurse. "Please…" Taking Grayson in my arms, he immediately stopped crying.

"Guess that was all he needed," a gal in white said.

Walking down the hallway of the Barton Memorial Hospital, I noticed a little plaque on the wall. *This wing donated by Elvis Presley—How appropriate*, I beamed.

Holding my new son carefully, I found a quiet spot in a large back room. We were all alone. Another nurse spotted us and brought a blanket. Softly, I hummed a little tune, as the baby drifted off to sleep. I was exhausted too. The birth had been early that morning and I was going on thirty hours without sleep. *My poor wife*, I thought; *Ten pounds and natural childbirth*. I had been in the room throughout the delivery and cut the umbilical cord. *So many stitches...*

Slowly, while holding the newborn, I made a bed behind a large ficus tree near a radiator. With the baby on my chest, I fell fast asleep too. Then I dreamed Grayson was communicating with me.

"Don't move, Dad—this is fine." It was like I had known this child my whole life.

It was nine o'clock in the morning when a group of nurses and one administrator woke us up in panic mode. "Thank God," one nurse exclaimed. "We've been looking everywhere for that child. We thought someone stole the baby!"

After the miraculous birth of our first son, I felt the need to settle down and become more responsible.

That year, we purchased a nice *Lincoln Log Home*, on three acres overlooking the valley in Verdi, Nevada. The California boundary line ran right through part of our property.

"We have dual State citizenship," I kidded.

When in town, we began going to a small neighborhood church nearby. *God wants to bless our little family*, I thought.

Grayson was walking and talking by the age of one. I was glad my folks were retired and helped with the childcare. For a time, my Mother-in-law, Cherie, stayed and helped out too.

Dad and Grayson loved to play 'teacher and student' at a blackboard, often trading roles and hats.

"Grayson knows how to calculate the number of transfats on the side of the cereal box," Dad said excited, "He loves trying everything new."

I concentrated on a music career hoping to be home more with our son during the day. Strangely, the music money was steady. Our band had bookings for over a year in advance. The business experience was paying off.

While many days were spent at home changing diapers, the travel beckoned. With a family alongside me daily, things were rewarding, but often very difficult. At least I wasn't just living for myself now. There is a song by the band, *Journey*, called: *Faithfully*. Some nights, I would sing this song with the line, *"The road ain't no place to raise a family."* What a truth this became. It tore at my heart when I was apart from the family.

Over the ensuing five years, I played music, *on and off* the road, with our own *New Country Band* formed with National fiddle champ, Valentino. We called the group *Valentino & Sol*, performing at fairs, Mississippi riverboats, concerts, casinos, on the Vegas strip, and swanky private affairs.

One afternoon we were paid handsomely to play for the owner of several casinos, Steve Wynn. It was a coming home party for his friend, Mike Milken, just released from prison.

As rich and famous guests sang along to *Beach Boys* songs, the party-life felt shallow for once. No one seemed happy.

"It's kind of ironic," our drummer Roger said on a break; "Our host has one of the best private art collections in the world and he's going blind…"

"He needs a faith healer," Valentino offered.

On the road, the only Bibles were in hotel room drawers. "Instead of attending church, we'll play a gospel medley each night," I reasoned, "There's quite a reaction to singing: *'Will the Circle be Unbroken'* in a big Casino.*"* But the circle of life would continue in a whole new way with more exciting news:

"There's another baby on the way!"

Another Birth – A New Heart

While performing the next month at the Nugget in Reno, I had an urgent call at two in the morning.

My mom called the backstage phone saying, "It's time to get to the hospital." There was urgency in her voice. My band objected and said I could not leave.

"Go after our next set is over, *or it's over,*" one band member said. The implication was that I would be fired from my own musical group.

"You must be joking," I replied, "What if it was your baby being born?"

I made one call to find a musician to replace me for our last show and hurried to St. Mary's Hospital. When I arrived at the hospital, my wife was in full blown labor, and no one was in the room. A nurse in the hallway said, "There are no doctors available right now—she will just have to wait."

"I don't think this baby is waiting," I replied.

The nurse became rattled and put a glove on to check, "You're right—she's over ten centimeters!"

Abruptly, the nurse left the room white as a ghost. I ran through the hospital to find help; riding the elevator to each floor exclaiming, "Baby on the way, we need help, stat!"

Finally, a tall older nurse said, "Honey, don't worry— in Texas we have our babies at home." Grabbing my arm, she pointed at the elevator and said, "Let's go."

Back in the delivery room, the Texas nurse threw a white smock and mask at me and said, "I'm gonna count on you to help bring this one in."

The nurse had me help by handing her linens and a tray of instruments. My wife pushed a final time and Nolan was born. Then the nurse steadied my hand while we cut the umbilical cord together. Handing me the baby, she instructed, "Clean him up and give him back to Mama."

Shortly the room filled with people in white coats. After being directed to the scale area, Nolan was cleaned up, and drops were placed in his eyes. Nolan weighed in at 7 pounds, 6 ounces.

Afterward, our OBGYN doctor showed up and asked for the chart. "You're late," the nurse told him. Annoyed, the doctor checked sutures and soon left the delivery room.

Later, I saw the Texas nurse in the hallway and she handed me the 'Certificate of Live Birth' for the hospital.

"We're signing on the doctor's line," she stated matter of factly.

Then while holding Nolan, I thought, *what matters is this little guy. And thank God for ten fingers and toes.* Once again I had a strange sense that I had known my son always.

Back home, I hugged Grayson happily and let him know he would meet his new brother that afternoon. Quietly, he comforted me, as I broke down, after 48 hours without sleep. I fell to my knees, praying for the first time in quite a while: *Praise You Father God, Thanks for a healthy Mom and baby, Nolan, and for sending that Texas nurse too.*

The Road Takes its Toll

When the local music jobs were not enough for full time work, we went on tour again. Traveling and the hard life on the road, took a toll. On the eve of our big break, after receiving some country radio airplay, with our song, *Too Many Ways to Say Goodbye,* our Band Manager, "Happy" Shahan, died suddenly at his Alamo Village Ranch, in Texas.

"How will this affect the European tour?" our guitarist wondered. Then, while driving from the funeral, Valentino and Gene, our producer, were in a devastating car accident. Gene landed in the hospital with third degree burns. Our dreams of Europe were dashed.

That week, my second wife moved out suddenly. *Maybe she wasn't ready for all of this—maybe with my wanderlust, I wasn't doing my part.* The bills were mounting and taxes were due.

Packing up my sons, our band found a job at the Oasis Resort near Las Vegas. The hotel provided child care.

I made it a point to take the boys swimming each day in the resort pool and visit historical sites.

On our last night, a Deputy Sheriff called me over to the side of the stage, in the middle of our show. "Sorry Eric," he said while handing me a twenty-page lawsuit for divorce. "She is suing for custody of your kids in a California court."

Just when I thought things could not get any worse, the following week I was pulled over in my Porsche near Reno, by a Nevada Highway patrol officer.

"I'm heading to play music at the Nugget, I said.

"There's a new *waste of gas law*," the officer replied, "you were accelerating too quickly."

The officer ran my driving record.

"You have an outstanding warrant for your arrest here in Nevada," the sheriff said, "You left the scene of an auto accident on the Mount Rose Highway."

"The other guy ran into my car ten years ago," I protested, "we went to the hospital before the police even arrived."

No mercy— the officer arrested me.

Cowboys & Indians in the Jailhouse

I spent the night in jail alongside the loudest, proudest and drunkest men around that night.

On one side of me was a large fellow, who said;

"Just call me 'Indian.' and we will be all right." The fellow on the other side was a tough looking cowboy.

How ironic, I thought: *it was a long way from playing cowboys and Indians as a child.*

"He got me arrested," Indian said, glaring at a fellow on the far side of me.

Being sober for once, I realized how out-of-control, sad, and empty it all seemed.

Then the Native American fellow on the bench leaned back in his chair and spoke to me in a low, deliberate voice, "Lean down and tie your shoe, if you know what's good for you." I did as I was told. A second later, he reached across my back and punched the large cowboy sitting on the other side of me.

Tex went flying across the holding area ending up on the floor unconscious. Several officers came and jumped into action, wrestling the big Indian down to my left.

Finally, a little black gal, the admitting officer, came around the counter and cried:

"Peace and quiet in here!"

The distraction seemed to work and both the officers and inmates settled down immediately. Sitting alone on that jailhouse bench, I thought, *Maybe I'm paying the price for all the previous times I should have been arrested. There were nights of drunkenness, gambling, lying and cheating.*

As the commotion died down, I snuck over to the admitting officer and pleaded my case. I related my sober tale and asked, "Hey, can I get a break here? Maybe show a little mercy? I didn't even know there was a warrant out." It was almost six a.m.

Then the petite jailer said, "Let me see about gettin' you a little mercy here."

By dawn, I was being released on my "own recognizance," where I agreed to deal directly with the court. That same blustery morning, with my Porsche impounded, I walked five miles to the courthouse in Reno. I would plead for more mercy from the notorious Judge Mills Lane. The judge had his own court TV show. He was also a known boxing referee, including Title Fights with Muhammad Ali and Joe Frazier.

"What's this? A new 'waste of gas' law?" the Judge laughed out loud, "That's a waste of my time law."

Deep inside I heard, *"Don't waste your life…"*

"I got no records on your accident," Mills said.

"It's the statute of limitations, your honor," I replied.

The judge broke in: "Are you some kind of arm chair lawyer?"—"You're still wastin' my time..." Judge Mills lowered his round spectacles and peered at me, "pay the administration fee and leave before I change my mind, son."

A few days later, I was in a courtroom again. I was fighting for equal custody of our two toddler sons. I won the first round in Sacramento by requesting to have the venue changed to Nevada. But a single father has an uphill fight. This would be no boxing match with a winner—all parties lose in divorce—especially the children.

Men with Cute Little Kids

Music was a great distraction from dealing with the courts and my personal problems. I looked forward to performing each evening.

That summer, I met a raven-haired gal who was also a Mom. "I'm happy to watch your kids, while you're at work," she said.

Men of divorce often think another woman is the answer for their small children. It seems that women are also drawn to men with cute little kids. Things moved fast for us.

"Are you fooling around with the babysitter?" our guitarist wondered.

After a trip back to Disneyland, we broke it off.

"Too many issues going on," I heard. It would be nine years before the sitter called again with life-changing news.

C.O.P.E.

Next to losing a child, I believe the hardest thing a parent will ever endure are custody battles. Mine were no exception. I began to witness bias against men through the process of my own court case. The court in Nevada, would not hear my case for a major parenting role. In court, there were many fathers losing the right to see their children for six months, or more, after a form motion was filed alleging abuse.

That night while performing at the Nugget in Reno, I made a new friend. "I would love to 'sit in' with your group on piano," the man said.

"Great—it will give me a chance to play a little sax," I replied. "Are you any good?"

Our drummer, Roger, assured me, "Not only is he gifted—he's the Governor! And a Medical Doctor…"

"Lieutenant Governor," the man corrected him.

After our show, the "Gov" and I talked late into the night about the broken court system in Nevada; especially concerning men and custody issues.

"There's one woman, who controls access to the Family Court Judges," he said, "She *hates* men." The Gov had endured his own custody battles.

"It's hard to cope," I lamented.

"That's it!" the Gov said, "let's start a council for men in this situation, called COPE."

Here I was in jail a few nights before, and now I was planning a council with the Gov. It was a *Zero to Hero* moment for once. After another meeting, we determined the acronym for "COPE" would stand for "Council on Parental Equality."

Shortly, we had twenty men meeting in a conference room at the downtown Lutheran Church. We began every meeting with prayer. The Dads took turns telling their woeful tales. It improved my own outlook as we counseled other sad Dads, organized meetings and assisted with legal paperwork. *Maybe my own legal troubles over the years, gave me the experience for this,* I realized.

After writing an expose article for the Reno News and Review, I received a call from the Gov. "I saw your article," he said, "the truth is getting out there."

Lost and Found in the Desert

Sadly, my second marriage had ended. Among other things, my life as a musician had proven too difficult for us.

I started studying to become a loan officer and financial planner. I also renewed my Real Estate Broker's license. But I needed money to pay court costs and attorney fees, *a last big music job*, would supply our needs for a while, I reasoned.

One sizzling July morning I traveled to the only 'money gig' I could find. I packed up my two small children again and headed to another resort-casino outside of Las Vegas. Daycare, or rather 'night care' for the children would be provided. I would be playing piano and sax with the old 50's group, "The Drifters."

Traveling through the most barren desert in Nevada, I took the journey alone with a baby and a three year old. Broke and without water, we became lost in the dark on the *Loneliest Highway in America*; Also known as the "ET" highway. Here I was driving all night just to make a Vegas show to replace a keyboard player who was fired for drunkenness on stage. It was 7 a.m. and over 100 degrees.

Then right out of a bad movie, my Mercury Wagon sputtered and died. *Just like when my family station wagon died on the way to California.* The broken gas needle had been stuck on a quarter tank. Now it showed empty. Just like I felt; *empty.*

To make matters worse, I had been experiencing a pain in my lower abdomen for several months. I closed my eyes and immediately passed out in exhaustion. I awoke a couple of hours later to the baby crying. There was no formula and the diaper needed changing.

As dawn was breaking, the distant sunlight funneled straight into our rear-view mirror. It cast a heavenly glow. I closed my eyes and said a silent prayer for help. All at once there was hope. I sensed there were angels all around us. There was a *"Peace that Surpasses All Understanding."*

Holding Baby Nolan, he stopped crying and started making musical sounds, even though his diaper needed changing and had no formula. Grayson, then a toddler, slept peacefully. What happened next, I can hardly explain.

I gave the engine one last try hoping there might be one last sip of gas to get us over the hill. The car sputtered and inched forward. I sensed loving hands pushing the car up the mountain highway to the crest. We reached the top!

A minute later we coasted downhill for ten miles, to the nearest town: Caliente, Nevada. *Caliente* meaning: 'hot.' Floating into the old desert town, generous folks provided food, gas, and some money for diapers and formula. There was enough gas to get us to the "Drifters gig." Later that same night I was playing the oldies but goodies, like *Under the Boardwalk* at a swanky Vegas resort, while staying in a pricey suite.

Before I had left for the trip, my Dad had given me an Og Mandino book, which contained a *Memorandum from God.* I would read this book on my outdoor breaks from the music. It helped to escape the cigarette smoke and casino noise.

One late afternoon, while reading outside under a large palm tree, I found the *Memorandum* at the end of the book. The letter was from God to me—or the reader. But I saw it as a personal revelation to me. One paragraph read:

Weep no more. I am with you...and this moment is the dividing line of your life. All that has gone before is like unto no more than that time you slept in your mother's womb. What is past is dead. Let the dead bury the dead. This day you return from the living dead..to a new life...

I remembered how God had just delivered us out of the desert. God would accept me back. He had never left me. I could become a salesman for Jesus! Tears welled up and began to fall on the last page of the book. My earthly father had penned these words to me, in the margin on the last page: *"You made it all the way through, son—"You can always make it through with God. Love you Son, Dad"*

I remembered the story of the Prodigal Son, returning to a forgiving Father who waited with open arms. *It would be hard walking back into a church sanctuary,* I thought. *This will take some time.* But God acted fast.

A Great Pretender

That weekend in Reno, I was backing the famed fifties band, *The Platters* and singer, Herb McQuay. Over the years, Herb had led decorated Military and large Church choirs.

During the middle of the Platter's song, *The Great Pretender,* I felt like a "pretender," myself: The words struck a deep chord: *Oh Yes, I'm the great pretender, pretending I'm doing well, lonely but no one can tell, I play the game but to my real shame...I seem to be what I'm not...I'm a great pretender...* The words blurred together and so did my vision, as again tears welled up.

Later that night, I bared my soul to McQuay at the *Sands* coffee shop: "I've been a pretender my whole life, I guess—

101

with women, business, vices—the only time I truly feel at home now is on stage."

With wisdom, Herb said; "Men often have a hard time revealing their broken places to anyone—but there's an answer." After a brief pause, he continued; "I need help this week selecting choir members for a Baptist Church here in Reno."

"Count me in," I responded, "In Chico we sang with a big Baptist choir at our Christmas shows."

It was more difficult than expected to select the Reno choir. Over one hundred parishioners came to audition.

"How can we say 'no' to anyone that wants to sing for God?" I asked.

Herb had the best solution. We formed three different choirs; Beginning, Intermediate and Advanced.

Later, McQuay took me aside giving more encouragement, "Your time is coming—keep writing—it's about words and music…"

For the first time—in a long time—I was excited to see what The Lord had in store for my life.

Finding Faith and Forgiveness

A Messenger Pigeon

Approaching middle age in the year 2000, I was a single dad with young children. Custody issues are often the most difficult consequence for the parents of divorce. I felt overwhelmed by life. After some success in music and Real Estate, the hard times seemed to play out daily. Lost marriage, financial woes and now my longtime band had split up. Moving back to Paradise California closer to my children and folks seemed like a better option. I had to break-away from the nightlife in Nevada. My old friend Greg Scott had safer musical wedding jobs waiting.

Then another old friend, Noble Spees, called my cell from a large Church where a revival was taking place, "This is where you need to be tonight," he said simply.

"I'm playing music across the highway at the Country Club," I said, "The Greg Scott Band."

"Take a break and come over," Noble replied.

Reluctantly, I drove to the conference. Walking into the large arena there were thousands of people. The main speaker of the night came right up to me through the crowd and grabbed below my gut on the right side.

"You feel it right here—don't you?" he stated, while squeezing my side hard. How did this man know that I had been experiencing a deep pain in that exact spot each night? I recoiled and stared up at the imposing figure who was a stranger to me.

"We need to get you some cleansing prayer," he said, placing a large hand on my shoulder. He asked for a spotlight to be shone on us. Then he called several folks over to pray for me. I was soon kneeling in the middle of a circle while several men and women laid their hands upon me praying. It was the music worship team. *Did they sense I was a musician?*

The speaker went back up on the stage with his wife, pointing to me saying, "I see a messenger pigeon, worship, and teaching; pay close attention to Chronicles—Chapter Twelve."

A Messenger Pigeon, I wondered, *why can't I be an Eagle?*

"You have a message banded tightly around your leg and you need to share it...Its one word."

Immediately the word *LOVE* came to me. After my few minutes under the spotlight, I dashed back to play music at the country club across the way.

As our band blared '*You've got to Change your Evil Ways,*' by Santana, I played the organ solo on autopilot. My mind was racing about what had just happened at the large revival across the street. I had a floating sensation. It had all happened so fast.

Dueling Pianos and Aneurysm

That summer, I still played a few secular music jobs for the income. Breaking old ties was hard.

My friend from *The Fortunes*, Steve Duerson, called one day and said we had a feature spot for "dueling pianos," at a new Indian Casino near Crater Lake, Oregon. "We each have fancy hotel suites too," he said—"in case you want to bring your sons."

One of *The Fortunes* hit records was, *"You've Got Your Troubles, I've Got Mine."* It was a sign of things to come.

Over that week, we *held our own* on the big stage, trading songs and fast piano licks back and forth. During the shows, we toasted the crowds with expensive bottles of bubbly and Bordeaux wines.

"Anything you want this week," the manager said.

On our way back to Paradise, we hiked by beautiful Crater Lake, the deepest Lake in the States. Over lunch, we planned a "Drifters Meets Platters," Concert at the Paradise Performing Arts Center, with Greg Scott II, already becoming a teen sensation.

Then on our way home by Mount Shasta, the fancy red wines caught up with me.

"My head feels like it's going to explode," I said.

"This is more than a hang-over," Steve said, "You have blood dripping from your nose." My piano pal was into a healthy diet and juicing, "alcohol constricts the blood vessels in the brain," he added.

"Never had a nosebleed," I said, as my head fell forward. The bleeding wouldn't stop. "Better call one of my doctor friends."

Stopping in Chico, Doc Creech had a neurologist come by. My head was still throbbing; even one ray of light was excruciating.

"Might have had a mini-stroke or aneurysm," the specialist said, "there's a little blood in your ear canal too."

After a few tests, the neurologist wrote a prescription and said: "A week of rest in bed, with sleep, lights out, shades drawn, homemade chicken soup and lots of water."

"It's either that or the hospital," Brev Creech, added.

That week while lying in bed, I listened to health stations on the radio. Dr. Joel Wallach with *Dead Doctors Don't Lie,* was illuminating. It would open a whole new world for me in the area of natural health. I never filled the prescription.

By the end of the week, I opened the curtains to a beautiful sunset over the valley. Squinting, I turned the radio dial to Christian pastors with life-giving messages. Names like David Jeremiah, John MacArthur, and Chuck Swindoll. I closed my eyes and just listened. Sitting on the deck, I remembered the man who had prophesied over me, calling for prayer at the Neighborhood Church conference. Now here he was on the radio! He was a known Christian author and speaker along with his wife.

Finding a Bible, I looked up Chapter 12 of Chronicles, as he had declared over me. I found it was about appointing the music directors during King David's time. I wanted to do better and stay away from drinking or dating for a while.

'I have to think of my kids,' became my motto.

Drifter's vs. Platters

"You recover pretty fast," my drummer friend, Steve Smith said, checking in on me, "Are we still on for the Drifter's vs Platters concert?" Steve was in our *Ammin' Jammin' Band* doctor group, and I was honored to have been a best man at his wedding.

"It's all set at the Paradise Performing Arts Center," I replied, "we're on the cover of tomorrow's newspaper."

The *Paradise Post* showed a "face to face" photo with the lead singers from the Platters 50's group and the Drifters band staring eye to eye with the caption: "Drifters VS Platters." The headline appeared like a Title Bout boxing match.

That month I vowed to, *live like a Boy Scout:* Up early with healthy juicing, an organic fresh farmer's market diet, exercise, and *NO* booze. It helped that the band member selected for the event were supportive. My parents in Chico helped promote the Luau Hawaiian Dinner before the concert. Tickets were, *All Sold Out.*

The night of the concert, our jazz quartet opened the show and then became the Headliners backup band. Greg Scott II, an *American Idol*, contender, joined the stars for the encore. *Finally,* I thought, *one in the "WIN" column. And I kept the drinking in check all week.*

Hired as the Calvary Church Music Man

That week I drove to speak before Nolan's third grade class for a, *What does Your Dad do for a Living Series.*

When the teacher asked Nolan if he knew his father's profession, he exclaimed, "My Dad's a Banker."

"I thought he was a music director and Realtor?" the teacher seemed puzzled.

"Well…he plays piano, but he's a banker, a *Coldwell Banker!*" Nolan was right; I had started working with the large real estate company. It would be weeks before receiving my first commission check.

One night, I prayed for income just to pay my child support. Two days later, a man called from out of the blue with a music job in church. The pay was exactly the same as my child support! I took notice.

"We need someone to lead the music team and choir," the Church President said.

Wow, this would be a great opportunity to keep making music after moving closer to the kids in California, I thought.

"I'll be there this Sunday," was my reply.

After getting off the phone, I felt conflicted. It had been a long time since attending church regularly. Now I was asked to be the music leader.

Calling my Dad, he reminded me about God's *GRACE*. I mistakenly thought self-sacrifice and my actions justified me: *Had I not helped with choirs and played music for veterans and widows? Had I not played music for the Disabled children? What about our Christmas Shows at Laxon Auditorium?*

Recently, I had realized my choices with women, alcohol, and truth had caused a separation from God. Not being able to get in touch with emotional wounds, I had learned how to put on a facade. A mask.

That Sunday, I was hired as the music director at Calvary Lutheran. The coming months seemed to go well. It was great to sing favorite hymns again; and I was encouraged to select newer Christian music. Shortly we had several singers, a guitarist, violin and flute. There were thirty members in choir for me to direct. When the call went out for a new pastor, I voted for the younger guy, fresh out of seminary.

"Let's add a *Taize Service* on Sunday evenings," the excited Pastor Rabe said. In the service, we sang harmonized tunes in languages like Latin, interspersed with readings, prayers and periods of silence.

Later, at my parents' home, I led another Taize service, introducing the old European style worship to several pastors from different denominations. It was a night of reverence.

After, Dad and I started working together, with the men from church, on a couple of homes for the Habit for Humanity charity. *A great fit for a Realtor*, I thought.

Horizons were expanding. It felt like a whole new day was dawning. But old habits are hard to break.

Dazed and Confused

When the new Indian Casino opened up in Oroville, our *Greg Scott Band* was hired for the Grand Opening Gala. It was right down the street from the church where I had recently become the music director. *What a great sign,* I thought naively.

The Saturday night opening came, and we were on the TV news in the big tent. Our band kept playing those old rock & roll hits until the wee hours of the morning. The free champagne kept flowing too. "Wine is good for the heart, right?" I often said. I had given up "hard" alcohol several years earlier, believing that wine didn't count.

Deep down I knew otherwise, remembering the throbbing pain in my gut. But that night my wine of choice was a Brut champagne. It proved to be brutal.

At three a.m. I left to drive home. Dazed, inebriated and confused, I pulled into the church parking lot down the road, barely able to drive. I managed to get my key into the lock of the church door, turn off the alarm system and pass out in the front pew. Sometimes I felt like my own worst enemy.

At 7 a.m. on that bright Sunday morning, I awoke in the church sanctuary, still feeling the effects of alcohol. Sheets of choir and piano music were scattered around me.

On my hands and knees, I crawled to the altar and mumbled: "Lord, please help me make it through this worship service and create in me a new heart oh God!"

I felt like a hypocrite when Pastor Rabe tapped me on the shoulder and said, "Nice to see you come early to pray before service."

Then the worship team arrived and helped to prepare the music for the day, where I muddled through two services.

That night in bed, I read Chronicles 12 once again: King David appointed musicians as, "Holy priests."

In the middle of the night, I woke up with a new song and wrote down the lyrics:

"Hold me Jesus, rock me Lord, let me come before You as a child adored.—Shine before me, light the way, hold my hand so tight that I won't go astray..."

Tears began to well up in my eyes as I wandered on the redwood deck, overlooking the vast Butte Valley, *"Lord, my life has been a mess—Help me change."*

A Man in the Camel Hair Coat

The next Sunday, during the middle of our church service, a tall thin man with long dark hair, walked slowly down the center aisle. He wore a long camel hair coat and held a large staff mounted with an eagle. Striking features...mid-thirties, but appearing much older at the same time.

All eyes watched, as he slid near me in the empty front pew. I was hesitant to look up at the man. But then I noticed his translucent eyes. There was a calm—a peace like I have never felt before. We sat quietly side-by-side. He signaled for something to write on. Someone from the row behind us handed me a yellow guest card. Then he smiled as I passed the card to him.

Then the Man in the Camel Coat wrote several indescribable words in what looked like an ancient script. Was this Hebrew or Aramaic? Was this man homeless? A Prophet? Was he here to give me a spiritual lesson? The man nodded and held the note below my eyes. Then handed me the message: The writing was otherworldly and I did not comprehend its meaning.

Right then our Pastor looked in my direction and nodded towards the piano. I had forgotten that it was time to play music for the prayer and offering.

The Man in the Camel Coat was making haste to leave, but I gestured towards the piano. He smiled and then lowered his head in a praying position, all the way on the floor.

Without forethought, I played the Hymn, *Nothing but the Blood of Jesus* singing: *"Oh precious is the flow that makes me White as Snow."*

After the song, I returned and sat by the man in the camel coat. With one look and without words, He nodded for the yellow card with the ancient writing; He wanted it back! One last time, I studied the precise writing more carefully. This time I got it! It said:

> *"Will you give Love always, with ALL that you have?"*

Will you give Love always, with ALL that you have?

I wanted to keep the card he wrote upon for proof. Still, I reluctantly returned the card. Then as our pastor prayed, I closed my eyes and saw a peaceful sea with a great light on the bottom of the ocean floor. I remembered hearing our sins would be thrown into the depths of the ocean when we ask forgiveness. *Forgive my past, Lord,* I prayed, *Let me follow Your plan for my life.*

Then the man in the coat stood, and we rose together from the pew. Without pretense, he gave me a big hug in front of the still-seated congregation. Holding up the tall cane with a carved eagle, he stepped decisively back down the middle aisle toward the large sanctuary doors.

Then this svelte, yet venerable man with a staff vanished. The church service seemed to end abruptly.

Afterward, an usher came running in from the crisp spring day and said, "When I let Him through the front door, I looked back and he just seemed to...disappear..."

"Our sins will be thrown in the depths of the ocean when we ask forgiveness.

When I started towards the exit myself, I became light-headed. I leaned back on the front wall for support.

As church members filed past, people asked me the identity of our visitor: "Was that one of your Rock Star friends?" some little old lady wondered.

One deacon said, "Maybe it was some homeless guy, probably needed some money for drugs."

My favorite comment was from a choir member who sat nearby him. She beamed, "His eyes were so sparkling—so filled with love."

Finally, Pastor Rabe asked me with one word to quiet everyone, "*Eric?*" he said.

113

"That was amazing; He was real…" I stammered and pushed out the door. I scanned the parking lot hoping the man at church might need a ride. But like the usher mentioned, it appeared *The Man in the Camel Coat*, had vanished from sight. I quickly exited the Calvary parking lot, driving back towards my hillside home on Storybook Lane.

As my car drove through the lush green Butte Valley, past a rainbow of new wildflowers, a rush of emotion fell upon me and I recognized a voice, a still small voice. It was a voice of comfort: *"See there on your passenger's seat, it's not empty—I am always with you."*

There it was—a program from that morning's service. When I turned the Church Bulletin over—on the front, in big bold letters were these words:

"I HAVE SEEN AN ANGEL OF THE LORD"

That night, while reflecting on what had happened earlier in church, I realized that more than anything, I needed to turn my life around from my own misguided ambitions.

In the middle of the night, I woke up after knocking my Bible off the bed. Grabbing it from the floor, I read:

"And the Angel of the Lord encamps around those who fear Him, And (God) rescues them." (Psalm 34:7)

Once again, I found myself out on the deck at Storybook Lane, as stars lit up the sky; I called out to the Lord. This time I just cried, "Thank you for saving me—I'm Yours."

Back in my room, I lit a candle and read Isaiah 44:22:

"I have swept away your offenses like a cloud; your sins are like morning mist. Return to me, for I have redeemed you."

A Dove in Paradise

That week came another transformative moment and it confirmed my recent experience; that God is always with us. There was an urgent call from my Dad. The folks had been watching my two sons while I was at work.

Dad said: "Mom is on her way to your home on Storybook Lane. We had a fire across the street from our house in Chico and two fire-fighting planes dumped a load of retardant directly on us. We were helping neighbors evacuate. The boys are okay, but we are all a little shook—*Red Goo* is everywhere."

Mom arrived with my young sons and we sat out on the deck. As they related the harrowing details of the fire raging around the Chico home, Mom broke into tears. I had never witnessed her sob like this. We were on the spot where I had cried out to the Lord, a few nights before.

Right then, the boys noticed a peculiar site down in the canyon. It appeared to be another small fire but it was flying through the air. Something was winding right towards us quickly through the trees. As it approached, we realized it was a snow white colored bird. *A dove.* The setting sun had reflected a bright golden light from the bird's wings. The dove circled in front of us putting on a dazzling display of aerobatics and landed on the railing to the deck.

"Don't scare it away," Nolan whispered.

I reached out and hugged them all—"See Mom, God sent a messenger to let you know everything will be alright." The boys decided to name our new pet dove, "Spirit."

A couple of days later, a friend who was a volunteer firefighter called me at work to say that a fire had reached the edge of *my own* property, "You had better get home right away," he said.

While speeding home, I tried to remain calm thinking about the dove hanging around our home all summer, seeming to watch over us. *She can fly to safety*, I thought. Now, the newspaper headline on my front seat read, *"All of the Butte Canyon Fires are Extinguished."* Turning up the driveway, I noticed a Fire truck from the neighboring town of Durham.

"We just happened to be passing by on a training exercise," the Captain informed me. "A power transformer blew out and started a blaze on your property—you better thank God we were right there," he said.

Wow! The fire chief was a man of faith.

That summer the spotless white dove comforted us every day. My sons would buy seed to feed her with their own pennies. We heard soothing sounds of cooing day and night. Often, in the early evening, while the sun was setting over the valley, the dove would circle our home and catch a bright glimmer of fiery sunlight on her wings. I smiled every time the boys called, 'Spirit.' I knew that trials were a part of life, but now I knew—we were not alone through them.

Discover the Rock

In autumn, I was asked to help with another church in Paradise. I would represent them as their Realtor to find a new location. 'Discover the Rock Church' had been meeting in the local movie theatre in town. Upon my first visit, the worship leader announced his retirement. Was the Lord leading me to help with the music, as well? By the following Sunday, I was leading the singing. I would continue directing at Calvary Wednesday and Sunday evening. It was best of all scenarios; *and a great way to stay out of trouble.*

The Rock Ministry was started by Norm and Donna Gardner. Norm had been with Family Radio, and Donna sang with our Worship team; an inspiring combo; powerful words and sweet music. My goal was for pure praise, including all ages with our music team. I remembered my old pastor Jensen's admonition, to *encourage other's talents.* Our team became diverse with young and old alike.

However, it was disconcerting to sing; "Jesus is the Rock," in a movie theatre and look up to see an *R rated movie* called *The Hot Chick*, advertised to begin at noon.

On Monday, I drafted an offer to lease an empty bank building for the Church. The property owner was in agreement. There was a special prayer gathering called. Then I submitted the case to the County Supervisors for approval.

"It doesn't look good," one supervisor told me. He was against the Church operating in a place, *meant for commerce*—"I will oppose this to the board."

The day of the final vote, the supervisor who was railing against the church was absent. They took roll call and someone reported he was, "quite ill." To take his place, a man walked in late and joined them. It was a Realtor friend of mine named Marino.

117

Pastor Norm touched me on the shoulder, "Will you talk on behalf of the church?" he asked. *Me?* As I approached the large stand, my friend, Marino, gave a reassuring wink.

"Instead of a bank vault, the church plans to open a *Community Food Bank*, in the vault there," I informed the Supervisors; "there is not one gathering place in town."

Then Pastor Norm simply said, "We have been called to help reach people there." After a short recess, the bank location was approved as a Church!

That Sunday, I was asked to lead the children's sermon. A toddler, who brought a toy guitar to play with our Worship team said, "I know Jesus, He is my best friend. He never lets me get lost." Little Alex was right…

"Jesus is my Superhero," I told the children, "I was lost for a while…" Before I could finish my statement a little girl chimed in: *"But Jesus found you and here you are!"*

"And that's How Jesus Saved the World"

A New Lease on Life

One early Sunday morning before the service, three of the rock pastors beckoned me to come with them. As we walked along the steep cliffs of the Butte Creek Canyon, one of the Pastors pointed to a singular cloud in the sky. It was in the shape of a giant trumpet. Suddenly the white cloud turned dark black! As we stood together with out-stretched arms, Pastor Don prayed, "Lord, I believe you are showing us, *The Trumpets have sounded over us!* We must turn back to You.*"

The following Tuesday, the twin towers fell in New York City. Rushing to our real estate office, I said, "Anyone that wants to go home can leave. Anyone that wants to pray is welcome to meet in the conference room in ten minutes."

After, I did not want to hold back my faith anymore. I recorded a CD of original faith based songs called *When Sunday Comes.* The song was an anthem about the change I believed was upon all of us. I related it to the Kennedy assassination as a frozen moment in history, when people's hearts changed. I believed the Towers held this same omen.

The title track, *When Sunday Comes,* had the well-known Frank Zappa drummer, Billy Mundy, featured on a military type of cadence. Before internet music was in vogue, we had thousands of hits on the song:

"Old Glory on the casket then Johnny salutes, the drummer drums the piper plays the flute. Old Glory on the casket, they can't take that from you... when Sunday comes we'll all know the truth."

"You really need to add a choir," Billy said. "The song deserves a choir—some fancy guitar too."

119

That week I met the Charvel Twins, who lived nearby in Paradise. Both were amazing guitarists. Immediately, we hit it off and started recording and playing live music together at churches and events. At half my age, Bob and Rick, *The Charvel's*, were inspiring to my faith. They both, "Loved Jesus and the Bible."

"You're like guitar angels," I said.

"If you lived with them you might think otherwise," their faithful Mom said.

Wayne Charvel, the twins Dad, was a well-known guitar maker. Wayne had invented the "hot rod guitar," design that the "stars of guitar" relished. It was commonplace to walk into their home and find someone like Eddie Van Halen, snoozing on the sofa waiting for his new 'Axe.'

Bob and Rick, the twins, were quite rebellious to the electric guitar family model, "We play only acoustic guitars," brother Bob told me.

The NAMM Shows

That spring, Wayne Charvel invited us to showcase in Anaheim at the NAMM Show. The annual event brings musicians together with the National American Musical Merchants. Wayne would be receiving a *Hall of Fame Recognition* that year. It was quite an honor just to attend in the company of the Charvels.

At the show, the twins received an "endorsement" to play Martin acoustic Guitars; often considered the best. The twins wanted me to try a system that displays the notes on a screen while a piano is played. Then while playing this new Yamaha electric grand, I noticed a large video camera aimed at my fingers. "Your feed is going live to a million square feet here at the convention center—largest meeting hall in the west."

Rick whispered in my ear, "Don't be nervous."

Afterward, one of the board members of NAMM asked, "what can we do for you?" I was never so happy to hear the Charvel Twins' response.

"They have all this metal and hard rock music, punk, and hip-hop—what about doing a Christian jam here on Sunday morning?" Rick Charvel said.

"Yeah, and film it too," brother Bob chimed in.

That Sunday began the *NAMM Worship Jam*. JBC or the *Justified By Christ* Band was also there. It gave me great hope sharing with these youth for Jesus.

Celebrating Discipline

On my way home from the music show in Anaheim, I picked up my sons near Sacramento and headed to the Bay Area. We were meeting my parents for another conference in San Francisco on the *Celebration of Discipline*, with author Richard Foster and the noted theologian Dallas Willard.

"It's about the path to spiritual growth," Dad said.

On our way through a side door the first night, my youngest son noticed the guest speaker, Dallas Willard, in a back office of the church. He was alone.

"Stop," Nolan said, "I want to meet him."

121

"This is for you," Dallas said, handing Nolan a copy of his latest book, "It's good to start young." Nolan was five years old. Afterward, we all took a walk on the Golden Gate Bridge.

In the morning, Foster and Willard, hosted a round panel discussion on prayer, fasting, meditation and the study of scripture:

"We practice these by finding ways to be alone, away from talk and noise," Willard said, "we rest, we observe—dare I say it—we stop and smell the roses."

Both sons rested their heads on my shoulders during the talk. *My life has been so hectic,* I thought, *it's time to slow down.*

Shortly, I would have no choice in the matter.

Dad and Mom on the Golden Gate Bridge in San Francisco

A Widow in Paradise

One morning I was on our weekly Brokers Open House tour, with our *Coldwell Banker* office in Paradise. Towards the end of the tour, the Broker, Steve Williams, asked if I would take a drive up to see his new listing in Magalia.

"It would be best to go alone," Steve said. "She just lost her husband." The older widow had listed her home with our company. It was several miles up the hill, and Steve worried that, "no one will visit her all day—besides—she might have some nice cookies for you."

As usual, Broker Steve was right. The widow had both fresh baked cookies and had been alone all day. No one had toured her distant home.

"I'm moving closer to my family," she said.

The widow described going through illness with her husband and a difficult funeral. She related the pain and said, "I hope my husband is in Heaven."

After an hour listening to her story of a faithful fifty-year-marriage, she began to cry. I reached for a Kleenex and handed it to her, feeling compassion.

"It will be better living closer to family when your home sells," was all I could think of saying. *I really blew it,* I thought. I had said one sentence the whole time. She later called the Broker to thank him for *"Sending such a thoughtful gentlemen."*

After leaving the widow's home, driving down the long Paradise Skyway to Chico, my cell phone rang to a voice filled with panic. The woman on the line said three words: **"It's your Dad."** Then the line went dead.

Death in the Family

I knew immediately that my own Father must have died unexpectedly. On the drive, my mind flooded: *Is Dad dead? —I had just met this widow, my Mom must be in turmoil now, Dad had given me a heads-up the night before...*

Arriving at my folks new home near the Chico Creek, I pulled up as the ambulance was pulling away.

The neighbor lady, who had called me in the car, met me at the door and said, "They did everything they could to revive him. His heart just stopped" *It was quick and hopefully painless for him*, I thought.

Mom was being strong, but was pale, and I called for their pastor to come over and pray with us.

I began phoning the family to give them the news. I tried to keep it together. Every call was filled with deep sorrow and pain. Somehow my visit with the widow earlier that morning had prepared me for this moment.

The week before Dad died, he had been working on a home nearby for Habitat for Humanity. While clearing off some roofing materials, a co-worker held a tree branch back for Dad to descend a ladder. Suddenly, the tree branch snapped right into Dad's face, knocking him off the ladder. Always stoic, my Dad continued working that day.

"He's been feeling off ever since," Mom confided.

The night before Dad died, my parents were teaching a class in their home on the Christian Disciplines: Prayer, Meditation, Fasting, Benevolence, Studying the Word. We had studied them at the conference the prior month. I could tell my Father wasn't feeling well that night. After relating the "Habitat falling off the ladder story," he said the doctors had given him a "clean bill of health." A week before, he had ridden his bike over ten miles in Chico.

At seventy-five, he was the oldest guy at the gym.

After the Bible study, Dad walked me to the car in his bathrobe and said something I will never forget, "You may have to keep an eye on your Mother now…"

We talked further, and then I questioned his strange comment, "You're okay, right Dad?"

"It's all going to be fine," He replied with a knowing smile. But I saw his pain and acceptance that he was right with God. When I drove away, we both had wet eyes.

That following morning, was when Dad died; it was right while I was meeting with the widow in Paradise.

Before taking his last breath, my dad, known affectionately as, "Dr. Tom," was outside in the garden tending the roses. Calling my good friend, Greg Scott—we made funeral arrangements. My singing pal, Greg, was also a mortician. The outpouring and support from family and friends was heartfelt and healing.

One of the deep wounding's for all men is the death of their Father. Dad was my best friend. Now he was gone.

Over the week, family and friends headed our way. I simply stayed at the home with Mom for the week, doing my best to help. During the wake, my sons were a great comfort to me. Nolan, at four-years-old, asked me to hold him up so he could touch Grandpa's head in the casket.

"Can I have a piece of Grandpa's hair?" he asked mortician friend, Greg Scott.

Greg found a pair of scissors and handed Nolan a small plastic bag, helping him snip off a lock of the snow white hair placing it inside. Seven-year-old Grayson looked up and said, "Grandpa's in Heaven now."

Late that night, I found the book *The Return of the Prodigal Son*, by Henri Nouwen, in the folks' vast library. In the middle of the story, I finally shed tears. I had come home to my own father's house. Now words leapt off the page: "From the deep inner place where love embraces all human grief, the Father reaches out to his children." That was Dad.

Aunts, uncles, family and friends, were coming from all across the Country. The funeral itself would be packed. So many people were calling; there would be a second service later in Castro Valley.

At the Memorial Service, Cousin Sue Smith from Fargo, sang 'I Was There to Hear Your Borning Cry.' Then she and Greg Scott joined with me in singing on a song I wrote for the memorial service called, Home to the Promised Land:

"Father take him to Heaven soaring into the light
Send your angels to comfort and give eternal life
Then the grandfather clock strikes a chime once again
Now it's time to remember this one who's called home
Take him home to the New Promised Land
Another life makes a page in the book of The Lamb
From "In the beginning" through Revelation
Take him home to the New Promised Land"

After the Memorial Service, one of his many professor friends mentioned Dad was the best 'Counselor with empathy' he ever worked with.

Later, when I asked him Dad's secret, Dr. Boehlmeir stated, **"Your father was the best listener I ever met."**

It made me think of the movie with George Burns and John Denver. At the end of the film, Denver asks Burns, in the role of God, if he will ever talk to him again. Burns replies: **"You talk; I'll listen."** And that is how I want to remember Dad. He had often reminded me to talk to my Heavenly Father. God does not promise us a pain-free life; He does promise to be with us through it all.

A New Mentor

Right after Dad's funeral, I would meet a new mentor. At a local coffee shop in Paradise, I noticed a big man reading a large Bible.

"Howdy Amigo," the big man said, noticing my interest in the beautiful, but well-worn book. "Do you know the Lord?" He questioned. After hearing my long tale of how I was a music director in Church, he asked, "Do you want to know Him better?"

"Right now?" I asked.

He opened up to the Book of Genesis. "We better start at the beginning," he laughed.

Roger was a Calvary Pastor who had studied and worked with Chuck Smith, the Calvary founder in Cosa Mesa. A former Green Beret, Roger Babcock and his wife Sandee started *Two or More Ministries,* counseling couples. They also helped direct a local Christian school.

Roger advised me to spend time with God every day by reading the Bible, "See you next week, Amigo," Roger would finish our study and coffee time.

A few weeks later, "Pastor Rog," and I traveled to other Calvary Churches. We would be stepping in to give pastors a break. Roger would be preaching and I would lead the music.

One Sunday in Davis, California two Iranian brothers joined in the music and gave their testimony. They both played several instruments with proficiency and sang. Their story was transforming. It gave me insight with testimony.

The two brothers from Persia told the story of how they had just lost their Dad the prior year, "Our dad was an Iranian Christian Minister under the Ayatollah regime, one said. He was brutally murdered by the secret police in Iran; taken into a field, tortured for two days and then beheaded."

Unexpectedly, many in the congregation came forward. Everyone started embracing the young men and praying.

"We tell our story to win souls for Christ," Amani, one brother said, "We have forgiven our father's killers."

"And our Heavenly Father compels us to tell the story of his Son," Pastor Roger finished with prayer.

"It may be that *unforgiveness* separates us from God more than anything else," Roger said, "When we are believers, God has already cleansed our past—we are free to move forward."

For so long I had not forgiven my exes. Now I felt freed to move forward in life. *I do want love again,* I thought.

7

Fools Rush In

"Fooled Again"

One Sunday, after leading music at the Calvary church, an older married couple approached me, "My wife knows a great gal who is perfect for you—she has her own business and goes to church," he said.

Jim sang in the choir I was directing.

"Are you playing matchmakers?" I asked.

"She's a stunner," his wife winked.

My parents had been friends with Jim and his wife for years, and I trusted them. He was also our family insurance agent. In the past, women often lured me in with, "speech seasoned with sugar."

Two weeks later, I was in the new gal's hair salon. Leaning me back in the chair, she started massaging my scalp seductively with a tropical shampoo. "I'm licensed as a masseuse too," she smiled.

After chatting further, she leaned over and said, "So glad to meet you—when do you want to get married?"

"Married?" I asked, "We just met."

When I went to pay, she winked, "I can't charge my future husband." Pulling out her appointment calendar, she continued, "I'm wide open in July. Let's mark down the second Saturday for a big wedding—I've never been married before."

"Maybe we need to go on a date before that—to make sure," I said, completely dumbfounded.

"By the way," she added, "I have four wild kids."

Later, on the golf course, my friend Greg said, "Sure you're not thinking with the wrong head? Remember the *Who* song: *I Won't Get Fooled Again?*"

"She's a "big Christian," I replied. This time I was *fooled* because she knew more Bible verses than me.

After a brief courtship and wedding ceremony, work and children dominated both of our lives. With our demanding businesses we rarely saw each other.

Since my last divorce, I was now, "out of the frying pan and into the fire." Each evening I looked forward to trying a new wine for escape. *Vintage wine helps cope with life's pressures*, I reasoned. Like the empty bottles lining the liquor cabinet, I always felt drained.

Sometimes we bury ourselves in *busy* to forget the deeper issues in our life. I felt a loss without seeing my young sons daily. I had masked my pain with another new marriage. This was my third.

Later that summer, my nephew, Ross Hertzog, needed a place to live after backpacking in Europe and it helped that he moved into our hectic home for a bit. *Thank God for someone that knows me*, I thought.

"Are you replacing your own children here?" Ross asked.

"Maybe you're a glutton for punishment," another friend Kurt Kearnes said, recording music one night.

"No, I'm a meathead—I just spent everything to buy this giant five bedroom home for the six kids." I would work even harder to pay for everything.

After speaking with my pastor pal, he reminded me that the acronym for *busy* is often, "**B**eing **U**nder **S**atan's **Y**oke."

Oh no, I thought, *that might be me.*

Once again I had made the mistake of jumping into a relationship before getting to know the woman, or her four children. Rushing into marriage—or a blended family is difficult for anyone.

"The devil hates a healthy marriage," Pastor Norm preached one Sunday at the Rock.

Between us, we had six children. Her older teenagers were often fighting. Our smallest ones were so impressionable. One afternoon, the older boy tossed my young son across the room, over playing a Gameboy. I made a pact to keep my own two sons away from the daily turmoil by staying with them in Chico at Mom's when I had custody. As a new widow, "Grandma was thankful to have the company," she said.

Poisoned in Paradise

Then back home in Paradise one evening, the melodrama reached a crescendo. While sitting down for dinner, my tiny step-daughter tugged on my pant leg and whispered in my ear.

"Don't drink your wine tonight, Daddy," she said. *She called me Daddy;* my heart melted.

Grabbing my arm, she led me to the garage and pointed to a bottle of radiator coolant.

"They put the cork back in too," she said, as a little wrinkle formed on her forehead, "but don't tell anyone I told you, or I'll get in trouble."

The older stepsons had tried to poison me!

My new wife at the time was less than sympathetic, "You must have really made them mad," she said nonchalantly.

It seemed like my sweet little step-daughter was the only one who cared about me in that house.

When my soon-to-be-ex did not want us to speak with a counselor or minister, I began searching for safer digs.

Why was it that I became enamored with women that were not good for me? Why did I plunge in so fast each time? Did I not have a roving eye and flirtatious nature? It was clear that I had not asked God to direct my paths before giving way to impulsive sexual desires, or considering the commitment of marriage.

Served a Summons at Church

Maybe I needed to make a few more changes in my life. I had rushed into another marriage, and once again, I would be served divorce papers on stage. The first time was while performing in Las Vegas. Now I was in the middle of directing the music at our Discover the Rock Church.

My wife of just one year had been filled with anxiety from the start; filled with fear over having a man as the head of the household. She had four children and had never been married. She was used to *calling the shots*—she wanted more control...she also wanted the big five bedroom home.

Then while singing, *I Come to the Garden Alone*, at the piano that Sunday morning, I was handed divorce papers by a big burly man, as the new wife looked on. Giving a blank stare, she turned abruptly and walked out the glass front doors. While our music team continued worshipping, I saw a few ushers rush out after her.

One usher returned and reported what had happened, "Right after she walked out the front door, she collapsed to the ground." Usher Ben had gone to help revive her.

As I drove away from church that day, I realized that I had been making women an idol over God.

"Watch out for the Jezebel Spirit," a Pastor friend cautioned; "Stay away from the lips of a wayward woman, as sweet as honey—but in the end as bitter as poison." It was a Proverbs, he said. *'Don't chase after women,'* I heard clearly.

Heimlich Hero

After witnessing my summons on stage, my drummer friend, Tim, advised me to, "Get out of that house right away!" Our worship drummer, Tim, had shared an amazing testimony in church about being delivered from drugs. He had, "survived several famous heavy metal rock bands."

Without hesitation, I moved the next day. Earlier, I had sold Tim and Mary their home and they now offered for me to stay in their guest quarters.

"She can have the house," I said about my soon-to-be ex-wife, "I'll keep the grand piano."

"Maybe you can have it annulled," Tim said.

It would be a long hard winter in Paradise, California.

Easter Sunday came and Tim and Mary surprised me with a BBQ at their home to "celebrate" my pending divorce. It had been *The Winter of my Discontent*, but seeing my sons on the weekends kept me going.

After handing Tim the steaks to barbecue, I retrieved the salmon from the kitchen.

"Fish doesn't take as long," I smiled.

Returning outside, I saw Tim bent over and clutching his throat. When I saw his face it appeared he was turning blue. Pointing to the steak with one hand and his mouth with the other, I realized Tim was choking. Since he was bigger than me, I jumped up on a step by the back door and grabbed him from behind. Taking both hands I made fists and pumped his stomach right under the rib cage. Then instinctively, I started pounding him on the back.

Right then Mary came from the kitchen, "Stop fighting you two!" as if we were a couple of kids horsing around.

Suddenly, a *HUGE* piece of steak flew out of Tim's mouth across the lawn! We both fell to the ground in a heap. Mary stood over us shaking her head, and Tim began laughing through the tears,

"You saved my life," he said, "You saved my life."

"What happened—were you choking?" Mary asked, bending down to help her husband to his feet.

"Good thing I just saw a medical TV show on the 'Heimlich Maneuver,'" I said.

I would not remain a 'Heimlich Hero' for long though. A week later my third divorce was final and so was the balance in my bank account.

Closer to the Sons

Seeking direction, one pastor, Levi Thunderburk, gave me great encouragement to: "Be there for your sons." I immediately moved closer to my sons in the Sacramento area, where I would have them throughout the summer.

We commuted four hours to church each Sunday, and the guys never complained. Grayson and Nolan helped with the sound board. Finally, I found a worship leader to replace me.

In Sacramento, I was offered a job in Commercial Sales and Lending and started grinding out a new living. It helped that I often worked from home.

Sons and Ringo's Drums in Maui

With one of my commissions, I received a bonus for a fractional condo in Hawaii. When summer vacation rolled around, my sons and I flew with Mom to Maui. We had a penthouse view of the ocean. There was sun, sun, sun.

Our first day in the Islands, eighty-year-old Mom came snorkeling with us. At one point she took her snorkel and batted at a wave, "Settle down there!" she said.

That night the guys and I snuck out to an arcade and saw Ringo's old Ludwig drum set on display!

Upon our return to the mainland, we were happy our new home had a swimming pool. It was humbling to rent after being a homeowner and landlord for so many years. My plan was to work less in real estate, lead Sunday worship and spend more time with the children. I would need to trust God with the finances. As those with younger children know, sleep would just have to wait.

Discovering Life's Idols

"See they are all false! Their deeds amount to nothing; their images are but wind and confusion." (Isaiah 41:29)

Holy Moley

Later on that summer, Nolan and I were swimming in the backyard pool. As a precocious eight-year-old, he noticed a dark spot on my arm.

"Hey Dad, I just saw this on the Discovery Channel," he pointed at my forearm, "I think I discovered a bad mole on you."

At the time, I just let it go, but a few weeks later while performing at a wedding with the singer Greg Scott, on a hot Chico day, he peered down at my bare arm dripping with sweat, "You better have that mole checked right away."

I noticed the mole had become much larger in just two weeks. With Greg's day job as a mortician, I took his medical advice to heart.

After a few calls, I heard there was going to be a health clinic with free exams. On Saturday, a Stanford doctor was walking by me in line and stopped in his tracks.

"How long have you had that mole?" he asked.

Immediately, he pulled me out of the line to study it. A few minutes later, I was undergoing tests for cancer. When the biopsy was returned, the doctor related that I had melanoma.

"A potential killer if it reaches the blood-stream." He wanted to operate on my arm immediately.

My first procedure went well, but the doctor said, "We just removed an epidermal layer and will need to go deeper."

Needless to say, I did not like the sound of this. I still needed to play the piano at church and had several other music events coming up that summer.

The second operation cut out more tissue deeper into the arm, "to increase the margins," the surgeon said.

At times, the pain seemed unbearable. The pain meds did not work well. They caused excruciating constipation and made me groggy all day. Unfortunately, I began self-medicating with more wine each day. For the first time, I canceled music engagements, except for the Paradise Church. On the weekends, I stopped drinking to be sober for church.

My "wino weekdays were justified," *There was an armful of painful sutures,* I reasoned.

One morning, I awoke and noticed my ride side had gone numb. Icky greenish-yellow ooze was dripping from my wound throughout the bed. My entire right shoulder had turned a deep purple color. After calling the Doctor, he told me to meet him at the surgical hospital right away. I knew this must be trouble. A friend drove me over.

"Too late for any painkillers," the doctor reported, reaching for a scalpel, "the infection is spreading rapidly throughout your body."

Two nurses steadied me on the exam table, while the surgeon worked to open my sutures with the scalpel. I began to pass out and he tried to keep me talking. After being revived a little, I noticed there was blood and puss everywhere.

I kept humming a song over and over in my head, to try and distract me from the pain.

After receiving more stitches—for the third time— I was relieved to find out that only the infection had spread. Not the cancer.

No more junk food, I thought; *too much pasta and pizza with the kids this summer.*

While recovering, an airline pilot friend brought me a bottle of pricey wine. "This is medicinal, he said. "Better than women."

Winning at the Rose Bowl

Then an amazing connection happened. I gave a recording of a song I wrote, "Hold me Jesus," to a physician's assistant, who passed it along to the editor of the magazine *Christianity Today*. He asked if he could share it with a Christian radio station. A week later the editor called again.

"The Reverend Billy Graham is an acquaintance of mine," he said, "how would you like to go to his Last Crusade at the Rose Bowl Stadium in Pasadena?" His wife wanted me to bring Grayson and Nolan.

"We're going to be sitting close to the stage and the four hundred member choir," he finished.

That weekend, we were at the famous USC stadium. This was the second time I was at a crusade of Billy Graham's. This time I wanted to make the most of it. It would be Billy Graham's last talk on the West coast. Billy began simply:

"Maybe you place money, work, or even science before God. Maybe it's drugs or drink..."

It hit me hard. I had put work, wine and women over God—they were my Idols—At that moment, I said a silent prayer of repentance; *"Lord, I repent of putting anything before You,—I'm so sorry."*

Then Graham talked about being "born again," and new-found faith. A Jewish named teacher Nicodemus had come to Jesus for the answers one night: *"You must be born again of spirit and water."*

Right after, the large crusade choir sang: "Just as I Am without one plea," and heavenly sounds flowed out into the warm evening air in Southern California. Over one hundred thousand people sang along. My sons were singing too.

I began to thank God for all of my blessings and vowed to do better.

Billy Graham gave the clear message of the gospel with the words of Christ: *"Jesus said, I am the way, the truth, and the life: no man cometh unto the Father, but by me."* (John 14:6)

Earlier that evening, at the Last Crusade, the opening prayer was given by the great modern crusader, Greg Laurie, from Harvest Ministry. A message that hit me the most from Pastor Greg was:

"Is there one thing in your life that, if God asked you for it, you would say, 'Absolutely not?' Is there one thing that, if the Lord required it of you, you would say, *'Anything but this?'* If so, then that thing, that pursuit—or that passion—may be an Idol in your life. Is there an Idol in your heart today? Is there someone or something more precious to you than God Himself? Any person, thing or pursuit that takes the place of God in your life will not satisfy. Let God be your satisfaction."

As people came onto the grassy Rose Bowl field, thousands of souls came to Christ. My own heart was renewed.

"I'm no Billy Graham"

In the morning, we returned home to Northern California with a fresh spirit. I finished recording my Christian CD of original songs. A week later, I was singing at the Herald Baptist Church where my sons were recently baptized. The pastor called saying he would be late, and asked me to give the mid-week message.

What? Me give an impromptu message—I'm no Billy Graham— that's for sure.

"Let's open the Bible to Acts," I said sheepishly. After rambling through fifteen minutes of, "We're all called to evangelize, and go forth to tell everyone the Good News," I said, "Let's just sing some more...here's a new one I wrote:"

> *"Hold me Jesus rock me Lord*
> *Let me come before you as a child adored*
> *Pure and simple, sweet and true*
> *Let your Love shine from above*
> *Through and through*
> *Hold me Jesus rock me Lord*
>
> *Shine before me, light the way*
> *Hold my hand so tight, I won't go astray*
> *Here me calling upon your name*
> *You're the greatest Father*
> *That a child will claim*
> *Hold me Jesus rock me Lord*
>
> *Hold me Jesus*
> *Rock me Lord on Holy Ground*
> *Let your name surround me*
> *It's a precious sound"*

When leaving the church, an older lady reprimanded me, "I heard your song *Hold me Jesus* on the radio, but I can't find the CD anywhere." She held both of my hands and looked sternly in my eyes, "Are you really going to get your mission going?—why are you not here every week with your boys?"

*Whoa...*she was right. I needed to work on balancing family and work time with following God's calling on my life.

One evening at a Chinese restaurant with my sons, my fortune cookie read: *"A two-headed dragon does not know which way to turn."*

Afterward, I worked out an arrangement to have our sons after school for a couple of hours; Nolan had been home as a "latch-key-kid." On Wednesday nights, we often went to the youth group at church together. The following month I opened a Concert in Paradise for Annie Herring, one of the pioneers of the *Jesus music genre*. It was my first solo outing.

I was still immersed in the Real Estate business but hoped deep down for more time for praise and writing music. Sometimes politics even stole my time. I prized, "being connected." As a member of the Exchange Club, I was in charge of arranging speakers for our luncheons.

New Twin Towers

That year I often felt conflicted, still placing work over God and family. At the peak of the real estate market, I had become involved in multiple commercial real estate ventures with a well-known Sacramento attorney and financial planner. Our offices in Sacramento, near the Capitol, had all the trappings of big success.

However, some days I felt a tug at my heart after leaving the Rock Church leading music. Was I seeking fortune through business instead of relying on faith? Our Franklin Hamilton firm was called to work on a large Twin Towers Construction project. I would help oversee the Real Estate development financing and consult on a sales program. The largest commercial and residential condo towers project west of the Mississippi. From the start "Twin Towers," sounded ominous.

After helping to arrange almost half a billion in loans for the project, and directing 400 pre-sales of the expensive condos into escrow, we were on top of the world. My eldest son attended the groundbreaking of the project with me. At one point in the ribbon cutting ceremony, I peered over to see Grayson standing by the Mayor and speaking with the architects of the Towers.

"Your son would make a great architect," I heard.

Then a Swiss banker said, "He knows politics too—let's go over and meet Governor Schwarzenegger!"

Coincidentally, the next morning I was asked by an attorney in my office if I would meet with Jerry Brown, the former governor. He was back running for office and hoped to return to Sacramento. The meeting was in Orinda, with several donors and celebrities. I asked two friends from Kenya to join me, after selling their Galt apartment complex. They were faithful Christians and promoted missions to Kenya.

After introductions, my Kenyan friends invited Jerry Brown back to Kenya, to meet their President.

"It did not work so well for me the last time I was there," Jerry grimaced.

Later, I found the media had trashed Brown for having an "undercover" relationship with singer Linda Ronstadt and taking her to Kenya. The word got out, and the press had a field-day. During the meeting, I asked Governor Brown about the time he spent at the side of Mother Teresa in India.

"How did you hear about that?—you're not an attorney, are you?" he surmised.

Thankfully, an old real estate client, Raiders quarterback, Jim Plunkett, came to my rescue: "Dinners on," he said. I was relieved to sit by Plunkett and his wife, involved in charities.

Afterward, people were leaving sizable donation checks. It was embarrassing to be empty-handed.

"Good luck with that big building," Jerry Brown said on our way out the door. *How did he know about that?* I wondered.

The Towers Tumble Down

Subsequently, our whole Towers project came crashing down. With the mortgage meltdown, it would become known as "The Real Estate bust of 2008." Four hundred penthouse buyers disappeared in a month, as financing dried up. Again, there was front page news. One of my partners was in a lawsuit over a million dollar commission.

"We were paid handsomely for selling the development site, but how can someone earn a commission on something never built?" our attorney reasoned.

"You're right. It's not my battle," I said.

The project left a huge hole-in-the-ground, at the Capitol Mall in downtown Sacramento. It left a crumbling cement foundation, where earlier the *"New Twin Towers"* broke ground. Millions of dollars in fees, equity, and profit, disappeared overnight.

My Kenyan friend, Frederick, met me later while clearing out our offices, "God has better plans for you," he encouraged. For now, I found two great Realtors to hang my license with in Carmichael. Bud and Rick were the Salt of the Earth and *1ˢᵗ Americans*. One day Broker Rick said:

"Choose your battles wisely, if you fight them all, you'll be too tired to fight the important ones."

President X

Later that month, I was at a fair with Mom and met another political candidate. McNerney was a professor, who knew Dad from Cal State, "I'm running for Congress," he said. His clean energy policy was enticing. It was hard for me to say, "no." A week later, I was campaigning again. With the real estate market meltdown, a change was welcome.

Late one evening in Elk Grove, I received a call from the Congressmen's office. It was pouring rain.

"Please join us at midnight for a private affair at the Executive airport for something quite special."

"It's raining cat and dogs," I replied. "What's so special for me to come out at midnight?"

"You will be with a U.S. President."

"Which one?"

"Let's just say 'President X." the voice finished.

Arriving quickly at the airport, I was escorted to the runway tarmac next to a Falcon 900 jet, by a man in a black trench coat, "What's your name?" he asked gazing down at a clipboard.

There in the pouring rain was Congressman elect McNerney. Standing at his side was former President Bill Clinton; "We're just refueling before heading to Vegas," he smiled, "wanted to meet a few of the locals."

Over the next hour, President Bill waived off umbrellas and tried to talk over the idle of jet engines. He laid out a plan to make the Congressman-elect an "Energy czar in Washington—we're gonna get *Hill* elected too."

I realized that Clinton was slurring his words. *Was he simply tired or tipsy?* I wondered. Hearing they had just come from a San Francisco fund-raiser, I decided it was the latter.

"California has the best wines in the world," Bill drawled. "Who's coming to Vegas?"

"I have younger sons at home," I begged off.

When leaving, I remembered back to my eight-year-old son coming home from school one day exclaiming, "The President is having sex under his desk at the White House!"

Arriving home at 3 a.m., I wrote a blog article about my midnight experience with, "Bill in the Pouring Rain," that was picked up by the Chicago Suns Times and Washington Post.

In the article I had reported Bill saying, "I have so much money now, I ought to be a Republican." Both newspapers picked up on the line.

Asked later about the midnight rendezvous, I said, "It gave me a different perspective on politics. I may be a bit of a braggart, but Bill beats everyone."

Later I wondered, *where's God in all of this? Had I not made idols of politicians, entertainers and even women throughout my life?*

Doctor Rocker Reunion

A week later, our old doctor-rocker band had a twenty-five-year reunion concert at the Sierra Nevada Showroom in Chico. My sons came with me. The night was filled with great healing for band members, as many of us had been through rough divorces. Now we had children and new lives.

That evening, singing doctor, James Farmer, asked me to play keys and flute with his Christian band at the new downtown plaza, in Chico. His sons played bass and drums respectively. Joining in was inspiring. *The JC Muzak Band* was fresh and original.

The older Farmer boys encouraged my sons to buy their own guitars, "I'll pay half," I said, in the old Soldahl tradition.

From Bust to Boon

That weekend, we stayed with old friends and clients, Dan and Margo Crotty. Mentioning my midnight experience with Clinton, my friend Mr. Crotty said, "We better watch the McLaughlin Report, to detoxify you politically."

Afterward, I began working on selling their Almond Ranch and processing plant. I had been drained both emotionally and financially, after the Sac Twin Towers deal imploded. Flying to Vegas myself for a real estate exchange conference, I started talking to a homeless man late one night, near the Hotels Valet parking.

"So I if I give you this money, will you use it for food, or go back inside and gamble with it?" I asked.

"Honestly?" he said—"I'll probably just lose it…"

148

"I've had issues with wine, women and gambling too," I replied, "the only thing that has helped me is knowing Jesus."

"There's a church around the corner," he said, "but I'm afraid to go in there."

Right then, a tall silver-haired man came up to us. His limousine had pulled up under the porte-cochere, but he signaled the driver to wait. "I heard what you said there," the older man smiled. Placing a hand on each of our shoulders, he continued: "Look, we are not our failures—things can change by helping others and finding out what is important."

"And that's not gambling or drugs, is it?" the homeless man said.

"It starts with being honest," he finished, "you're both on the right track." Handing us tickets for another conference, I saw the man's picture on them; it was the noted motivational speaker Zig Zigler.

Flying home I thought about faith, family and finances. Things can change fast in real estate with the right motivation.

After the Crotty's Ranch sold, I helped facilitate a 1031 exchange for a large Capitol City office building near the Sacramento Mall. His sister, Betty Ann was a great manager.

"Selling real estate has been a series of *Ups and Downs* for you," my Broker Bud said, handing me a fat commission check at the closing—"that's like selling dozens of homes."

"My personal life has had its ups and downs too," I replied. Then with one prayer, things changed dramatically.

True Love Found
(Finally)

A Match Made in Heaven

After years of trying to get things right on my own, I said a prayer one morning:

"Lord, I have really done a bad job in my relationships. I don't even deserve another wife. Please forgive me for my past with women. Lord—If it is your will for me to remarry, please choose her for me. I've done a lousy job picking the right one."

That same week, God brought me an earthly angel.

Eric & Elizabeth: The Love Story

We found each other on a famous Christian site. Her profile said: "I am passionate in my faith for God, my two daughters, creativity and dark chocolate." The lead words in my profile began: "I am most passionate about my Faith, my sons, writing and creating music." I also mentioned that I "loved dark chocolate."

150

We both listed our favorite book—after the Bible, of course as *The Road Less Traveled.* We are, *definitely a match made in heaven,* I thought.

With "eHarmony," we grew to know each other even before we met. The site leads matches through their, *likes and dislikes, open and closed end communications* and long phone calls. We had our first date in Walnut Creek. It was her Birthday week and the night was romantic. I never wanted it to end. We even danced a little around a restaurant. We were the only ones left at closing time.

A Match Made in Harmony Heaven

On our second date, we met halfway in the river town of Isleton and played a little golf. I was *hooked* by more than my bad golf shots.

On our third date, I drove her to the doctors' for a colonoscopy. The doctor was surprised this was only our third date, and Elizabeth trusted me to see her through the procedure.

"I want to get to know her, inside and out," I said.

After, the doctor stated she was in, "perfect health."

"She's a perfect healthy ten," I replied. She was smart, beautiful and we held the same values. Best of all, she was giving and kind; at ease talking to the school board on behalf of her two teenage daughters; and comfortable talking to the homeless on the street. My sons adored her from the start. Most importantly, we shared the same faith in God.

On our fourth date, I took Elizabeth sailing on Lake Merritt, in Oakland. I wanted to show off a few of my old sailing skills.

"This is a piece of cake compared to sailing on the Bay," I said confidently. In the center of the lake, I told the story of how my Dad had proposed to Mom in a "rowboat built for two," on a lake in Minnesota, "Dad offered her marriage or a long swim back to shore," I winked.

Now after breezing around the smooth waters for a bit, I realized there was no motor to take us home. Then sailing back towards the dock, the winds picked up and we came barreling at the pier. *Oh no, I had forgotten to take the sails down!* Quickly, pulling the rudder, the boat turned towards the dock and we slammed into the end of the berth. The jolt threw us backwards and she landed in my arms.

"That was really fun!" Elizabeth said, "And exciting..."

"You're quite a catch," I said, a little rattled. *She has no fear,* I thought.

On the way home, we took a detour to the largest cemetery I had ever seen. We drove high in the hills overlooking the Bay.

"My daughters learned how to drive here," she said somberly, "there is something I want to show you…"

Suddenly the car stopped. I was staring at a small gravestone with the inscription: "Here lies Baby Stephanie."

Then Elizabeth dropped a bombshell: "I'm responsible for killing a baby—*my baby*," she said with tears.

"I had a stillborn baby. I was drinking and overwhelmed during the pregnancy…"

She's not a big drinker, I thought.

At the time, I dismissed her guilt, "Oh, don't blame yourself," I tried to comfort her; "I heard my Mom lost twins, after too many radiation exams."

Kindred Spirits

We continued like most couples newly in love. In fall we visited the Villa Tuscana Winery in the romantic Shenandoah Valley for wine tasting. The following week we sampled varietals in Sonoma. Most dates involved dining and Chardonnay. The homestead where I grew up in the Bay Area had a small vineyard—my sister was an "enologist," at an award winning winery in the Napa Valley for several years. "Wine is life, according to Thomas Jefferson," I stated.

One day a Native American fellow on the street asked us, "Why do you think alcohol is also called 'Spirits.'"

He followed with: "Those kinds of 'Spirits' are bad news." But the personal news in my life was wonderful.

Elizabeth and I fell deeply in love. Shortly, I proposed on one knee in front of her friend, a retired nun, who raised a glass of champagne toasting us. We bonded nightly with bottles of cab or chardonnay. Over the years, alcohol was like "liquid courage."

As a songwriter, who once co-wrote a tune called "The Balance of the Bottle," and slammed shooters on the road with Charlie Daniels, I had given up drinking liquor in the prior century—wine doesn't count, right? Often I had fooled myself, having a glass, or two, or more with most evening meals.

My cardiologist had said: "The redder the wine, the better the wine…" We were fooled by the modern myth of wine-worship.

"It's like medicine for the heart," I rationalized to others, "Experts cite resveratrol and all those great antioxidants"— *never mind my poor liver.* Many nights I went to bed with that nagging pain on my lower right side. Many mornings I awoke groggy.

One night Elizabeth become angry, after drinking in an old Saloon, "We're fuming over nothing," I downplayed it.

It took *Premarital Christian Counseling,* to move us through our issues, forgiving each other for past relationships and poor life choices. We always looked forward to singing, dancing, swimming and attending church together.

Married on the Bay

On August fifteenth we exchanged vows in a beautiful ceremony aboard a decked-out boat on the San Francisco Bay. There were sixty loved ones and a large crew. My brother, Daniel, performed the ceremony after becoming ordained online. He recited Corinthians 13 and our favorite scriptures including, *"A threefold cord is not easily broken."*

We vowed to love God, each other and our children.

Exchanging Vows with Elizabeth on the San Francisco Bay!

At the time of our wedding, my brother was taking chemotherapy with stage four colon cancer, "I really wanted to be the one to marry you," he said with a heavenly glow.

As the sun was setting behind Angel Island, the windsurfers, sailboats and Golden Gate served as our

155

backdrop. For my vows, I looked deep into Elizabeth's gorgeous amber eyes and said:

> *"In giving all of myself to you,*
> *I promise to pray with you continually.*
> *Moving closer in mind, body, spirit and soul,*
> *Always rejoicing in our language of love.*
> *Lifting each other upward, our hearts into one.*
> *In giving ourselves to each other,*
> *We will become soul mates on a forever date:*
> *Best friends, partners, lovers and holders of each other's hearts.*
> *You are a precious bright light to me, Elizabeth.*
> *Beauty is passing,*
> *But a woman who loves the Lord shall be praised.*
> *The heart of this husband will always trust you.*
> *And I will always truly love you..."*

Then Elizabeth spoke her handwritten vows to me and my heart melted. All I heard was, *"Our love is forevermore."*

New Family

One of the blessings of my new marriage was gaining two new daughters. Jennifer and Kate were both in high school and very talented. Each one had feature roles singing and acting in plays.

They were both stars on the soccer team. Kate excelled in tennis and Jennifer was a soloist in choir. They had also gone on mission trips with the church to Mexico and Africa. Just great gals; I was so happy to have daughters.

My new wife's parents, Bob and Mary Ellen were as good as it gets. Mary Ellen played and had taught piano, while Bob, a retired doctor, sang in the church choir and loved to golf.

My two new brothers-in-law, Don and Mark, were both Eagle Scouts growing up. Each had given us heartfelt toasts at the wedding. They were family men and examples of a life well lived. Elizabeth also had lots of awesome nieces and nephews. On the wedding cruise, there was true family harmony.

Soldahls and Logans on High Seas

We left the morning after our reception for a Maui honeymoon filled with sun, sand, snorkeling, dancing, and singing too.

Later at Christmas, Elizabeth and I led a "Christmas sing-a-long," at the folk's home in Santa Barbara. On Christmas Eve, I sang with my new Father-in-law in their large church choir. Red robes too. Then on Christmas Day there was golf with the family in perfect weather. It was all exhilarating.

Fire Sale Home and Faithful Neighbors

Living back in the Bay Area after our wedding presented challenges. There were children in two towns. While lying in bed at night, we often heard gunshots from nearby Oakland;

"And we live in a nice neighborhood," Elizabeth said. Then showing real faith, we purchased a home that had been gutted in a fire. It was a demanding remodel in Elk Grove.

Our next door neighbor, Rich, was the Pastor of St. Peter's Lutheran Church just down the street. Karen, his wife said, "We have been praying for two years for a Christian couple to buy the vacant foreclosure home next door and fix it up—and here you are!"

They would become good friends. Later, we moved from the Bay Area to Elk Grove and joined the church. We were excited to be involved with the music and worship there.

One day, Pastor Rich leaned over the fence, like "Wilson," in the old TV show Home Improvement and gave sage advice to expand our horizons. Would we be interested in leading a *Truth Project* class in our home after remodeling?

"Hope you're handy with tools," I said.

"Not unless it's with a pen in hand," he replied.

Living on the other side of the Eddy's, was another pastor. Phil and his wife Krista, had sweet young children. Our other neighbors, *the Naef's,* were *big on family*. It was nice to live on a faithful street.

In the fall, Elizabeth and I campaigned together for the Presidential election. After the vote was in, we were facilitating *The Truth Project* class in our home. It opened our eyes that God's Politics are in favor of caring for the poor, the widows, the creation and the unborn. *Infinite love wants what is best for another person.* Sometimes the morals of society are opposed to this. Previously, in the Bay Area, we had issues with the public schools teaching poor values. We were thankful Grayson and Nolan were attending Bradshaw Christian High School, near our home.

Later, we saw Franklin Graham speak in person: "Sometimes we have to vote for the: *Lesser of two heathens,*" he said, "We need to stay involved to make a difference."

My understanding of politics changed that day.

"From now on let's campaign for Jesus," I said.

Heavenly Hot Tub

One Sunday afternoon, Elizabeth and I were relaxing in the hot tub. "I've never been baptized by immersion under water," I said, "my parents had me 'sprinkled' as a baby."

"Me too," Elizabeth revealed.

Right then Nolan came outside in his swimsuit. Nolan and Grayson had previously been baptized together in a large tub at Herald Baptist Church.

As Nolan stepped into our spa, I asked him if he would baptize us together, "We've never been dunked before."

Then one at a time, our son leaned us backwards under the 103 degree water. "I baptize you in the name of the Father, and Son, and Holy Spirit," Nolan said. He was twelve

159

years old at the time. We didn't know then that Nolan would become a preacher someday.

Breaking the Curse

Although I believed God had granted me a fresh start with Elizabeth, there was some marital soul searching left to do. I did not want to make the same marriage mistakes as before. Looking back, I realized both parties are responsible for the failures in marriage, but the man needs to be willing to go to battle for his bride. Many of my most painful marital memories were buried for years. One day, we prayed for God to *show us everything.* It was a lot to ask for.

In my case, I needed to consider past relationships, before there was to be a closer relationship with God leading to further growth in life.

The night after our *show us everything* prayer, I awoke suddenly out of a nightmare, recalling many sordid details of my past relationships with women. It cut me to the core. Over the years, it was easy to say, "It's all *their* fault."

An entire list emerged of the vast wrongs I had done to my ex's and the pain I inflicted, or suffered, as well.

Recalling a Dickens novel, like the "Ghosts of Christmas Past," I reflected back on my prior relationships.

For years, I had played the blame game. For years, I had been exonerated in the failed marriages, by playing the victim. In truth, I had broken vows. Often through overwork; I was rarely home. *Besides,* I thought, *I had lustful thoughts and flirtations with other women; sometimes even more.*

At 4 a.m., Elizabeth and I talked about my dream and past marriages. I asked for her forgiveness. Then we got down on our knees and asked God to forgive us for *all* of our past marital woes and relationships outside of marriage. We made an agreement not to talk about exes, finances, or issues with kids while in the bedroom.

"Please Lord, break off the marital curses and bless this new marriage with Elizabeth," I prayed simply. Right then a powerful picture formed in my mind. Again, I saw a loving Father holding out his arms to a returning son.

New Retreat Ministries

After heartfelt talks with Elizabeth, we wanted to take on the world in a whole new way together. So we planned a series of Christian retreats in Prayer, Meditation, Movement, and Music. We held a weekend retreat at the St. Columba Retreat Center along the ocean, near Point Reyes California.

Several close friends joined us including my Mom. I played flute during walks touring the Stations of the Cross. The views overlooking the Pacific Ocean were inspiring. There were centering prayers based upon scripture. At sunset, we sang praises by candlelight.

But God had some more pruning to do in our lives.

Upon returning home, we were in for quite an awakening. The enemy of God always wants to thwart growth in spreading the Gospel message. A friend had foretold that *we might be headed for trouble*. We had recently sat with a friend at a church picnic, who told us to, "Pray out the demons of sin daily." Her name was Kym, a Japanese 'born again believer in Christ.' She provided a simple prayer:

Dear Lord, please cast away demons, drowning them in the deepest ocean. Pour the healing, loving blood of Jesus over me. Thank you, Amen

What a strange prayer, we thought at the time...but began praying this simple prayer each night.

A few days after returning from St. Columba, we would both be *"Floored."*

Floored

It was just past 3 a.m. when I awoke to a thump and the faint sound of her sweet voice: "Honey, I need you...Oooooh my stomach..."

Without hesitation, I jumped out of bed and bolted downstairs. My wife was sprawled out on the hardwood floors of our Elk Grove home. It was a scene from another world. I wondered if I was still dreaming. With her face contorted, and eyes rolled back, strange gargling sounds were coming out of her mouth. I instinctively retrieved the tongue from the back of her throat.

Earlier that night, before falling asleep, I had read a scripture about demons, *"Lord even the demons are subject to us in your name!"*

Now Elizabeth was on the floor slipping into unconsciousness. I moved to sit her up as she writhed uncontrollably. *Am I losing my new bride?* I thought— instinctively I prayed out loud addressing the demonic spirits, "In the name Jesus, leave!" She had stopped breathing.

162

Holding her head up, I pressed my lips to hers and mustered a deep breath…once, twice; three times I breathed oxygen.

Then I cradled her and prayed in a *heavenly prayer language.* Words followed—"Lord God, please deliver my wife and drown these demons in the name of Jesus."

Finally she opened her eyes. Rolling over on the floor, she began vomiting, burping, and making retching sounds from every opening in her body. I knew a huge spiritual battle was ending, *Thank you God,* I thought.

Then with clarity she spoke: "Right before I passed out, I thought about alcohol as a cancer in my stomach," she said. "I think it was purged out," she finished.

As I carried Elizabeth back upstairs and tucked her into bed, I sensed we were starting over. There was a new light about her, like a new born infant. I cleaned her up and wanted to hold her in my arms forever. There was a genuine peace about her.

"Sweet dreams, my love," I whispered.

As she drifted off to sleep, I nudged her to make sure she was okay. With eyes closed, she placed a finger on a verse in Ephesians: *"And do not be drunk with wine in which is dissipation, but be filled with the Spirit…that He might sanctify and cleanse her by the washing of the Word of God…"*

Maybe Elizabeth was taking the hit for both of us, I thought. Maybe God had done a mighty-work in response to our prayer: *"Lord cast away any demons from us and drown them in the deepest ocean."*

For so many years, I had turned to intoxicating drink.

Dramatically, the desire for drinking was taken away from both of us that fateful night. *"He who is in you (the Holy Spirit) is greater than he who is in the world (Satan)."* John 4:4

But there would be temptations to come.

Brother Christian

A few days after our *Floored* experience, my friend, Christian, from our real estate office, invited me over with several investors. This group had also played poker into the wee hours before. Most of the guys went to church. *Sort of a picture of my life in two worlds,* I thought, on the drive over. I was planning to stop by for business and forego the booze.

Our gang of office buddies was there to discuss buying another building. As business talk subsided, the party escalated; the meeting sojourned to a discussion over the best wines. My friend and "brother Christian," had a self-admitted problem with drinking. But he was the first to pop a cork. The other men there were Catholics, including two lawyers.

First, trying to steer the conversation to faith and being *Floored and Delivered*; no one wanted to hear about my exciting night. I mentioned giving up drinking. But there is a pack mentality with men and our will is weak. After a little cajoling, I took a sip of a catchy Zinfandel, appropriately named: *The Seven Deadly Zin's.* At that moment, I told the fellas I needed to leave.

"I'm quitting drinking unless it's for communion," I said abruptly. My Catholic office mates raised a glass to toast me before breaking out the poker chips.

Then Christian walked me to my car, "My brother died in a car crash—I was driving drunk," he confided. "I, I should have gone to jail for a long time," he said through the tears.

"Maybe God wants you to quit drinking too," I said; "We can be a support for each other." Christian looked back with longing as he disappeared back into the poker party.

That evening I called my Green Beret pastor friend, Roger, who advised me to read *Psalms 1*; even before I told him about that night with my poker pals.

"It's about hanging out with the wrong crowd, Amigo," Roger said, "sometimes we have to find new company.

After our floored experience, I started researching scripture. It became the basis for my book: *Spiritual Firepower, Unleashed*; finding there is a continuing conflict in the spiritual realm, the invisible world, between God's loyal messengers and the demonic hosts of Satan. But the love and blood of Jesus will win out over the enemy.

"The Earth is the Battlefield where two Kingdoms wage a war for the Souls of Men." (Author unknown)

The Language of Heaven

One morning, I received a unique phone call at my real estate office. The man was a Spanish speaking pastor, originally from Peru. I fumbled through mediocre *Spanglish* until he rescued me.

"We want to buy the church," he said in a thick accent.

"Do you mean the VFW Hall I have listed for sale?"

165

That afternoon we were signing paperwork on the old Veterans of Foreign Wars building in Sacramento.

Pastor Castillo tested my Spanish speaking skills further: "Somos los Ancianos de la Iglesia," Meant: *We are the Church Elders*. Several stalwart men laughed at my puzzled response and then formed a large circle.

"They want to pray with you," the Pastor said, "we will need to raise a lot of money for this."

The building had been sitting vacant, and there was ominous looking graffiti on the walls.

"These symbols are from the devil," one elder said, "God wants to restore this to a Holy place."

Over the course of the afternoon, we walked from room to room and around the four-acre perimeter of the property. The men stopped to pray over the property often.

Then the prayers of these faithful men came to fruition. With more faith than money, we asked the seller to help finance the purchase. He loaned the church more than they requested. When the City denied the permit, we found a loophole: The zoning was approved for a non-profit meeting place, if it included a thrift store and daycare center. All three endeavors were thriving by summer. Pastor Castillo began a local radio program and started broadcasting church services to thousands in South America too.

Then another big blessing came to the *Iglesia De Christo Nuevo Pacto*; Church of Christ.

"Hola Senor Eric," Pastor Castillo called another day; "Someone gave us a big revival tent!"

166

Over the summer, an old style *Spanish Southern Revival* took place in Sacramento. When I joined them for praise music at the Revival, it was beyond words. I just kept smiling.

Afterward, the Pastor called me to the front: "Un 'angel de la Iglesia," he said, "You better learn better Spanish, Eric,—"it's the language they speak in Heaven!"

Mixing Marriage and Money

Putting our heads together one day, Elizabeth and I decided to buy, remodel, decorate and stage "Fixer Uppers." After the real estate market crashed, I no longer waited for the phone to ring with eager buyers. Together, we started buying properties and renovating. We combined my wife's interior design experience and my real estate expertise. We would be breezing through several profitable projects. One of our largest endeavors in Elk Grove was a five bedroom three bath Mediterranean gut job. It was on one of the nicest streets in town and our costs far exceeded the modest budget.

Three weeks later we sold the Tuscan home at another Open House. A Kaiser doctor paid, "almost full price."

"My children just love the tiny house in the backyard and I love that organic garden," our nice new buyer said. Later she invited us to a costume party to celebrate their new home and meet the neighbors.

But the joyful mood of that week would end with sad news. My brother Dan's colon cancer had spread to his other vital organs.

Love will be made Manifest

After hearing about my brother Dan having cancer, I remembered meeting a Spirit-filled Pastor named Dean. While talking to our men's group one night, he had stopped mid-sentence and stared at me intently. His first words sounded strange, but I did not forget them:

"God revealed to me that love will be made manifest through your brother's illness." Pastor Dean caught me off guard. I had been through my own bout with melanoma cancer earlier. I had a couple of deep scars from basil cell breast cancer too. *Maybe Dean meant some friend or brother at our Church,* so I glanced around the room. I was wrong.

Now here it was, a few years later, and my older brother, Daniel, was gravely ill with colon cancer. This was the first time someone in my family had life-threatening cancer. Thankfully, our family came together during times of crisis.

Family dinner honoring Dan at Center Street

Joy through Adversity

The morning after meeting my wife, Elizabeth, for the first time in Walnut Creek, I drove my older brother, Daniel, to John Muir Hospital for chemotherapy. Stage four colon cancer. He had gone through one period of remission and now was back in chemo. After being delivered from my own melanoma cancer, I hoped there would be healing for Dan. But my cancer was nothing compared to this.

The day my wife first met Daniel, he was in front of a church congregation giving the lesson of the day, reading from scripture. Dan beckoned us forward to sit with him. Later that morning, he took us on a tour of the *Our Savior Lutheran Church*, in Pleasant Hill, first heading to the patio gardens overlooking a rushing stream.

"This is my peaceful place," he smiled. "I come here to meditate and pray."

Daniel must have been in a tremendous amount of pain at the time, but never complained or expressed a negative attitude.

The first memory I have of my brother, he was singing in the choir at our palatial church. The Boys Choir all dressed in white robes. *They sound like angels from heaven,* I thought. I wanted to run and join them. But now my brother was fighting for his life.

In cancer treatment, Dan had signed on for a new radical interferon procedure, in hopes that this may lead to a breakthrough for others someday. Having a scientific background, Dan knew the risks.

After receiving the intravenous drip, into a portal directly connected to his heart, Dan sent the nurse to find me to come and sit with him.

"You don't have to stay for the whole time," he said, always considering others.

"It lasts most of the day." Then he smiled and said, "Before you head out, tell me how you're doing these days…Have you written any new songs?"

He introduced me to everyone receiving treatment and discussed cancer options. It seemed he knew everyone getting chemo and empathized with their story. It was then I determined to devote each Friday to spending time with my brother.

Before our Father died, he had given each of us children the book, *Tuesdays with Morrie*. It described one journalist's experience with his dying mentor. Now this was playing out for us in real life. Usually, Dan and I would be working quietly out of his home in Concord, California.

"Let's take a walk," Dan would say, "we need to get the blood moving."

His devoted wife, Jerolyn, would often pack us lunch. Dan never complained. On our walks we discussed family, friends, music, sports and our hikes together in the Sierras.

One day he reminisced about being an Eagle Scout. Dan's final requirement was to build a large signal tower alone for the Los Nochas Camp. The tower was to be used to relay and receive messages with a U.S. Ranger Station, during wildfires.

After Dan spent all week constructing the tower, the entire troop gathered for the dedication. My bare-chested brother was covered with a terrible sunburn.

The Scoutmaster then proceeded to push and shake the tower, enlisting help from several other Camp Administrators, until the whole wooden tower came toppling down. Boy was I mad at that Scoutmaster. What a calamity. Dan returned home late the next evening.

Before heading to a much needed shower, he reported the outcome of his Eagle project: "Man!" Daniel said, "It took me a week to build it the first time and I did it better, the second time in one day."

Dan had endured until the end. He had endured the humiliation and physical pain. This was a test of his character; a test to see it all the way through. My brother knew about hardship and perseverance.

"Let us run with endurance the race that is set before us." (Hebrews 12:1)

The Lord Gives, the Lord Takes and Gives...

Several months after Dan endured final treatments, the family gathered around his bedside at the end. We all told him how much he was loved. My Sister Christine began singing *You are my Sunshine*, a favorite song while traveling in *Van Europe*.

Then Elizabeth leaned in close to Dan and whispered, "Soon you will be in Heaven with Jesus," He managed a smile with bright blue eyes. Light seemed to enter the room, and Dan weakly pointed to all four corners.

"Angels," someone said. Then Dan drew his last.

"I have fought the good fight, I have finished the race, I have kept the faith." (2 Timothy 4:7)

The night after my older brother, Daniel, died of colon cancer, we had an amazing thunderstorm with over 1200 powerful lightning strikes. We felt God was near and were exhilarated—not afraid—much like my brother would have been. With lightening striking around us, Elizabeth and I planted a "carnival rosebush," that would bear hundreds of colorful roses every year.

The day after Dan died, I awoke to a fresh new world. There was a sweet small voice on the phone. I had never heard this quiet voice before and yet; it sounded so familiar:

"Hi Dad—This is your son, Paul…"

10

Family Miracles

"Behold I make all things new." Rev. 21:5

Paul, the smallest apostle...the biggest miracle!

That remarkable morning, a young boy, was calling me from a neighboring state.

"I saw your picture online, Dad," Paul said, "I saw my brothers Grayson and Nolan too."

During the call, Paul said he was nine years old. I immediately knew this boy was a part of me. It was like hearing my own voice when I was his age. I realized that I was not dreaming when I literally pinched myself.

I heard another powerful voice inside say: *"The Lord gives and the Lord takes away."*

173

Picking Elizabeth up that afternoon, I broke the news, "There's a new child in our lives." After the shock wore off, my wife said, "I always wanted to have more children— I had even thought about adoption or fostering before. But I didn't really expect this…"

But God had my own progeny in mind. His name was Paul.

Immediately we called a Christian counselor. We needed wise direction for our family and marriage. The next day we talked to Paul and his Mom, arranging to meet them.

Shortly, there was an amazing reunion at Mills Park in Carson City. Paul came running across the grass to meet us. The day blossomed into a joy-filled picnic with over forty family members and friends.

"You have the same true blue eyes," his Grandma said.

With Son Paul 9 years old - meeting for the first time

174

Paul would come to stay with us several times that summer—and become a big part of all our lives.

When my Mom first saw a picture of Paul, she asked, "Where did you find that photo of your Dad, as a boy?"

Elizabeth was my heart of hearts in all of this; faithful to the Lord's words: *"Whoever receives one of these little children in My name receives me."*

Paul was in fact my own son—confirmed with a DNA test. On our first solo outing together, nine-year-old Paul hopped out of the car at a roadside stop and climbed right up the side of 100 foot granite rock. Reaching the top in record time, he raised both arms in 'Victory.' *Adventurous.*

Besides computer skills, Paul was very musical. The Lord was so faithful to bless a middle-aged sinner like me with such a pure and sacred gift. Over the next few years, our new son was a bright light in our lives. Always ready to help out and gifted with caring for the young and old.

As a teen, Paul began singing in the chamber choir in High School and running the projection for our Worship Music at church. Some Sundays he joined in singing with the Worship team. In July, we stopped at the shores of Lake Tahoe and his older brother, Nolan, baptized him in the crystal blue lake.

"It's not going to be easy," Nolan said, right before leaning Paul backward into the icy waters, "Sure you want this?"

"Yes—I do," Paul answered.

Right after, there was a flock of white birds that flew directly overhead and started talking to us, "They're saying, 'good job – good job!'" Elizabeth exclaimed.

All of our children and family members welcomed Paul, understanding that he missed years with us. One night, I mentioned to Paul that I was sorry to have missed so much of his youth.

"That's all right," Paul responded, "I know we're making up for it now." When I asked him about his faith, he said, "I know God is real, I found my own Dad."

Love, Logic, and Family

"Train them up in the way they should go."

Elizabeth and I settled into a wonderful married life with great communication between us, but blended families are difficult. We had four teenagers at the same time! We sought out Christian counseling and then began teaching parenting classes ourselves.

My Dad, the professor, used to say, "We often teach what we most need to learn ourselves." So we organized a "Love and Logic" parenting class. In order to get kids to change, the parents need to change their own behavior first; then give expectations with clear boundaries and consequences.

Late one night, after spending hours video gaming, one of our sons came out of his bedroom and said, "I just want to kill someone…" We realized this was no joking matter. In fact, we noticed that young males did the school shootings, apparently addicted to first-person-shooter video games.

Advice from a Basketball Star

That week, after a Youth Group meeting, a friend stopped by our home with the guest speaker, who was a basketball player with the Sacramento Kings. Ducking under the doorway, I surmised Sean was almost seven feet tall.

Sean Smart was both a solid believer and 'smart' fellow with my sons. He took one look around the home and said,

"Look, your sons are probably on computers and gaming in their bedrooms right now." He was right. Sean took a long deep breath and continued, "First thing I did in my home when I realized the severity with this, is to move all the computers into a common area of our home.

"How does that help?" I asked.

"We now know what's happening in their life online," Sean replied, "going online is limited to after homework and just an hour on a school day."

Parenting and Porno

One evening in our parenting class, a distraught mother told us that she found her sons had discovered, "the gateway to pornography" through many online gaming communities visited by her teens.

"It's one click away," she said. "Many teen boys and young adult men no longer find the need to date."

Her husband continued: "Their needs are met by porno or online relationships—like social media and multi-player video games."

We started to see that teens were no longer developing face to face social skills, due to these online addictions. I had been exposed to pornography at a young age, with magazines. We recognized our children were "one click away," on their computers and even cell phones. One helpful book a Pastor friend gave us was *Every Young Man's Battle.*

With *Love and Logic,* we discussed: *Loving parents; train their children 'Up'* instead of talking *'Down'* to them. They give options to their children instead of telling them what to do.

Parents give love through empathy, "I know it's a bummer, but your room is quite a mess. I will be happy to give you a ride after it's clean." The key is to raise children that are responsible and independent: I found myself saying: "I only argue on Thursday's at three o'clock!"

Making their own Decisions

In High School, Nolan and Grayson both joined the Golf Team. Nolan started an "Accountability Club" for the guys. He wore a promise ring, to be accountable to God for his actions. He was the, "Self-appointed President of the club." Nolan even attended the prom with a date renting his own limo.

Later on, son Paul was selected for the All State Choir, where they sang in Anaheim visiting Disneyland.

"I don't know how I could make it through school without the singing," Paul mentioned, "It's a stress buster."

Grayson, attended Trinity Western University near Vancouver, Canada. He had met with a counselor on his own receiving a generous scholarship.

That fall, we flew to BC Canada. During lunch on 'Parents Weekend,' with the University President, he said, "Trinity Western gets an 'A' rating in academics but a 'D minus' for Pubs on Campus."

That spring, Daughter Jenny graduated from a U.C. and sister Katie graduated a year later from Loyola, both with honors. After graduation, we heard the best news given to parents, besides having grandchildren; the girls each found great jobs. Both had spent time on missions, building homes and orphanages in Mexico and Africa, for the poor. We were thankful both Jennifer and Katelyn had sung with us. Even their choices of boyfriends made us smile.

"We're hoping for grandchildren!" Elizabeth said.

"I heard Grandchildren are the 'Reward you get, for not strangling your teenagers,'" I chuckled.

With the Logan Family in Santa Barbara & Son Paul too

Birthday in S.F. with my wife, Nolan, Mom Flo, Jennifer & Kate

The 'I Believe' Concerts

My wife and I had previously planned to put on several Faith-based concerts together; sharing both personal testimony and singing new original gospel songs. The afternoon of our first "I Believe Concert," my side started to ache; I had a hard time standing up. Preparing to leave for the church, I doubled over in severe pain.

"It's my gallbladder," I said.

Elizabeth and I had both found new life and freedom after giving up drinking; however, consequences may remain from previous behavior. My gallbladder would often act up.

In a flash, my wife ran two doors down to find our friend and neighbor, Pastor Phil Fuller, who came to pray over me.

Phil brought healing oils and a heartfelt prayer: "Lord, you are the God of all restoration. Please heal my brother and friend, Eric. You are able to do all things. We know you are able to heal him right now." *Awesome neighbors*, I thought. Soon we were out the door heading for the concert.

Arriving at the church, Elizabeth also asked Pastor Steve Lundblom to pray over me. In a quiet area of the sanctuary, we knelt and prayed together. Spontaneously, Steve pulled out more healing oil and touched my forehead. "It's in the book of James," he said changing tone, "Let's do this!" Steve finished, pulling out his Fender Stratocaster guitar.

My gut pain improved considerably. Gathering all of the concert members, we stood in a circle holding hands praying together. Singer Cindy Woodrum set the tone, "All powers of darkness must flee now—Satan, you are *NOT* welcome here!" *Not too bad for Lutherans*, I thought.

When the concert started, the Holy Spirit came. I forgot about the pain in my side. *Praise is a great healer*, I thought.

Elizabeth shared her testimonial, focusing on love, healing, and forgiveness. Then I related my own life story of failed marriages, false idols with work, alcohol, celebrities and redeemed by the grace of Jesus; thankful for sobriety, married bliss, children, worship music and spiritual growth.

"It's *God first*, marriage, children and *then* business and work," I mentioned. "I am *SO* Grateful—"If God can forgive *me*, He can forgive anyone."

I started to choke-up when mentioning my brother dying from cancer. His widow, Jerolyn, was sitting with our family.

Heading to the piano, I sang *Jesus Loves Me.* "Thanks for paying for all those piano lessons, Mom," I finished.

The concert ended on a high note, with everyone holding hands and singing: *Amazing Grace my Chains are Gone.* Mine were. More *I Believe* concerts were planned for the future.

Deeper through the Trials

That spring, life blossomed even more when Pastor Eddy and I began a weekly prayer time together. It helped to be next-door-neighbors and I was rarely late.

"God's seeds run deep," he reminded, "keep praying for your children—my parents always prayed for us."

One morning I asked Rich what had taken him deeper into ministry. Nolan, had talked about becoming a Pastor, "Our son said he would love to 'work just one day per week like you,'" I kidded Rich, knowing he was going 24/7.

"It was Bible Study Fellowship," Rich responded, "each year is spent studying one book of the Bible."

A week later, Larry Davidson, approached me at St. Peter's and asked if I would consider playing piano for a large men's non-denominational Bible gathering known as: *BSF*

"It's been going for fifty years," Larry said.

Monday nights I looked forward to playing piano, singing hymns and studying with leader, Ed Law. Son Paul came a few times. Each year the study focused on one book of the Bible. Several times I felt honored to lead our group prayer.

Suddenly, prayers turned to my wife. She had non-stop bleeding due to a benign fibroid in the uterus.

11

From Hospitals to Praise

"She Could Bleed to Death"

Over the past couple years, Elizabeth had endured that *menopause phase* of life. Now I was washing sheets three times a day due to her heavy bleeding. We started seeking various medical opinions. There were many tests and procedures. Not one doctor could figure out how to stop her perimenopausal bleeding. We would once again be crying out to God with **"Knee Mail."**

One night, I walked in on my wife in the bathroom and it looked like a crime scene. Blood was splattered everywhere!

"No…" Elizabeth moaned softly, as she sat up in bed at two in the morning. We looked down at the Frisbee-sized bright blood spot on our white sheets. I whispered in a daze,

183

"You okay honey?"

"Yeah, just heavy bleeding again, all over the white sheets," she replied heading to the bathroom.

I heard her moan and ran to the bathroom. Blood was pouring out of her like a faucet.

This is really bad, I thought. I helped sit her against the window for a few minutes as life-blood drained. I noticed the skin on her hands and thighs were pasty white, anemic.

"We better call your doctor," I said.

Suddenly, another gush of blood splashed everywhere. Red dots speckled the tile floor around her and drips of blood stained her legs and feet. She moaned and then a few tears slid down her cheeks.

"Maybe we do need to go to Kaiser E.R.," she said.

Calling my father-in-law, Dr. Robert Logan, I asked, "What's the worst that can happen here?"

"She could bleed to death," he said, sounding alarmed.

"Pedal to the Metal"

"I feel faint and lost a few pints of blood, maybe quarts," she stammered. Her bleeding would not stop. Quickly, I grabbed her sweater, some black sweats, her purse and black clogs. Helping her put on the clothes, she wrapped a towel between her legs like a diaper and we hobbled to the car.

When I asked if we needed an ambulance she said,

"No, just go 'pedal to the metal.'"

Her seat was tilted all the way back, so she would not faint from blood loss, and her feet were on the dashboard as we sped on the back roads, arriving in record time to Kaiser South Sacramento. I ran to get a stretcher, as she had once fainted in a wheelchair before.

Wheeling her into the E.R., things seemed to be calming down until she asked for a bed-pan to urinate. The nurse said she could go to the bathroom down the hall, so I helped her walk slowly, step by step. Immediately, the hemorrhaging started again, this time even more blood poured out; *Splash, splash.*

She quickly dropped to the to the tile floor and passed out. I began calling out,

"Stat! Stat! Code Blue!!!"

In great haste, a group of doctors and nurses assembled to help lift her from the red and white bathroom tile. Most of the tile had now turned a crimson color. We rushed her back to the gurney.

"She needs a transfusion," I blurted out. Her blood type is "O Positive." In a matter of minutes, she was hooked up to an IV, oxygen, and an "O+" blood drip. *My time hanging out with the Doctors back in Chico was helping here,* I thought.

Elizabeth looked at my frightened blue eyes and squeezed my hand one last time, feigning a weak smile before drifting off. She appeared angelic with translucent skin. There were no longer any worry lines on her face and for a minute I thought the worst—maybe she was gone. Leaning in close, I could hear no breath at all. With the heart rate monitor hooked back up, there came a faint heartbeat. *Thank God,* I breathed. Closing my eyes, I prayed, "Please Lord, please, bring her back." A moment later she awoke with a faint smile.

Two days later, Elizabeth had a new type of embolization procedure to cut-off blood flow to the fibroid. It worked!

Recuperation at home in bed for a month gave time to read, write and reflect. Her bleeding was finally gone. We both rested. And rested. *And thanked God.*

Lumps and Bumps

Right after thinking all was well with health, my wife noticed a lump on one of her breast and asked me to check it.

"Your nipple looks funny too," I said.

Immediately, we went to her doctor for tests.

I have been told the hardest news for a woman to hear is that they have breast cancer. Her doctors wanted me in the room during the consultation. My wife's doctor said, "I have news from the biopsies. I am sorry to have to tell you, it is invasive breast cancer. There are four tumor masses in the right breast and three in the left. I'd like you to schedule a mammogram and then we will discuss options for surgery."

The doctor had informed us that she had invasive breast cancer on both sides. My wife started shaking.

"Elizabeth, we are here for you," her breast doctor said. "Call me anytime. With your faith you are a bright soul. I have goose bumps right now," Dr. De Young finished. *Quite a doctor, she had goose bumps for my wife.* After, we took a long walk by the lake in Elk Grove and I tried to comfort her.

Our culture places so much emphasis on that part of the female anatomy. Throughout my life, had I not made "Boobs" a False Idol? More slang words were created for breasts than just about anything else. There are even restaurants named after them like, *"Hooters."*

Calling my wife's Dad, for more medical advice, Dr. Bob was realistic, "Look, breasts are external," he said, "just tissue you can do fine without."

Following this, we scheduled mastectomy surgery.

Breathe *"Faith"*

The night before surgery, our next-door neighbors Pastor Rich, and Karen Eddy, invited us for dinner. They had a visitor staying with them from Ohio, Pastor Curtis Lyon, who heads the American Lutheran Churches. His wife had survived breast cancer several years before.

After we ate the delicious home cooked dinner, we invited everyone over to see our Tuscan style remodel. Seizing the moment, Pastor Curtis grabbed my guitar and I joined in on piano. Suddenly, we were singing and the room filled with spontaneous spirit-filled worship together. The elder pastors laid hands upon my wife, praying for successful surgery. The Holy Spirit was ever present in that circle.

Pastor Curtis looked at my wife intently and said, "Dear Elizabeth, I pray *'faith'* over you. I pray that you have faith in God to get you through this. *Faith* that you will be healed. Breathe, Elizabeth—Breathe Faith. Faith, Faith, *Faaaaith…*"

We began breathing, *"Faith, Faith, Faith…"*

As I held her in bed that night, she whispered, "I believe I saw my breath as we stood in that circle breathing, *Faith, Faith, Faith...*'" We were being prepared for her cancer surgery - slowly washing our hearts with *Faith.*

Double Mastectomy

It was 6 a.m. at Kaiser South Sacramento as our pastor and his wife came unexpectedly to the hospital and prayed with us. *"Dear God, we pray for Elizabeth as she goes in for surgery. We pray for the doctors, nurses, and for peace. We pray for all of the cancer to be completely removed through this surgery."*

Then, I helped roll her gurney into the operating room. When she awoke from the surgery, I was by her side and took her hand, "I love you Sweetheart—it went really well."

She blinked her eyes and her numb body slowly came back to earth. She was alive. I leaned over and kissed her.

After prayer and research, we chose natural healing without chemotherapy and other recommended pharmaceuticals. The decision **not** to have breast implants also seemed right. While researching breast reconstruction, we discovered that implants could hide future cancer. They also may become very dense from scar tissue and adhesions, like a hard ball.

"Breast implants often have to be removed or replaced every ten years, as they can rupture or deflate," my plastic surgeon friend and bandmate had said; "I made money putting them in and more money taking them back out."

"We live in a plastic world," Jimi Hendrix sang.

After Elizabeth's surgery, the Winter Olympics were on the TV one night, "You have a sexy ice skaters body now – It works for me," I said. Thinking about my past with marriages and women, I thought, *This time I'm not running.*

"Thanks for sticking with me through all this honey—you're my hero," my wife smiled.

"You just get better, so that I can take you ice skating." It was good to hear her laugh again. I laughed out loud myself reading at bedtime: *"The wicked run away when no one is chasing them"*… (Proverbs 28)

Overcoming with Praise

During Elizabeth's recovery, we began singing together each evening and Elizabeth started glowing with health!

That week we planned more concerts. In summer, we combined with three church groups for a "Lovestock" Concert in the Sacramento Land Park. Sons Nolan and Paul ran the sound system. Nolan gave an impressive faith-filled talk beginning with a prayer to Father God: "Daddy—Abba, we love you…"

The sixties theme had many faithful folks dressing in colorful attire. Our worship team transformed old pop songs such as *I'm a Believer*, and *Love One Another Right Now.*

We closed the Concert singing the Doobie Brothers, *Taking it to the Streets*, with faith-based words, imploring the crowd to spread the "Good News." We felt called to share more music and ministry.

Faith on Fire

"It does not require a majority to prevail, but rather a tireless, minority keen to set brush fires in people's minds."~
(Samuel Adams)

In fall, we worked on defining our mission. We hoped to spread the Gospel message through our music and writings with concerts, books, and teaching. We named our new Ministry: *Faith on Fire.* We took to heart a key verse of Scripture:

"Be prepared to give an answer to everyone who asks you to give the reason for the hope you have. But do this with gentleness and respect." 1 Peter 3:15.

Elizabeth and I combined our approaches in reaching others. Besides performing music at Churches, Concert Halls, Senior Centers, Schools, Parks or anywhere they would have us, we found several ways to witness or discuss our faith. My wife often used the direct approach by sharing her testimony or handing out little Bibles. We would give *The Little Bible* out to the folks we met on the street, those we worked with or talked to in stores or restaurants. It helped to ask questions.

"What are you doing Sunday night? Want to come hear some Christmas music?— an invitational approach. Would you like a CD of some new songs?" With a service approach, many organizations need help delivering food, shelter or clothing. We love, "Love Inc." This is a Sacramento based Ministry for the needy and homeless.

With Nolan's help, we started a *Faith on Fire*, website and developed a series of music concerts.

That Christmas, teenage Nolan, sang for the seniors at Mom's retirement center: "*Chestnuts roasting on an open fire...*"

"Well, it does have the word 'fire' in it,'" we laughed.

Refugee Reunion

"Hi Eric, this is your old friend, Khoi!"

The phone was glued to my ear. It had been twenty-five years since seeing my Vietnamese pal, Khoi. After comparing notes on family and catching up, we made plans to meet. We soon became like brothers again. Khoi had worked for the Attorney General's office and done well, having two children and a long-term marriage to his sweet wife, Kim-Loan.

"So sorry to hear about your brother," Khoi said, "Dan was always nice and showed me computers."

Over that year, we worked together on an investment property and remodel project. Khoi had invested in Apple Stock!

"Khoi and his wife are enjoying the crafts fair at church," I mentioned to Elizabeth.

"Maybe they can hear us sing too," she said.

Afterward, they invited us to their beautiful home in the Bay Area. We celebrated with Vietnamese food and Christmas cookies.

"Bring your Mom," Khoi said, "I want to thank her for having our family stay with you when we fled Vietnam."

Another Heavenly Reunion

At year-end my sister called: "Your piano teacher, Ruby Pappas passed away on Christmas Day." Growing up, she was also Paul's Mom; my best buddy. Ruby was so encouraging and always had a welcome smile. The most accomplished organist and pianist. At my brother's funeral, her husband, Gordon, had Ruby listening to my *Grace Notes CD* on headphones. "Hope I didn't make too many mistakes," I had said.

"She just keeps smiling," Gordon reassured me.

At Ruby's memorial, the entire Pappas family honored her by playing music. It was so good to see my old friend Paul and his wife, Gretchen. I was glad they met Elizabeth.

"We have a son named 'Paul,'" I mentioned.

There were many old friends I had not seen in years; including my old next-door neighbor and sail boating partner, Ric Smith. He was now a deacon and leader in church.

The Awesome Light Band members were also there along with wives and many old high school friends.

"What a great reunion remembering Ruby," I said in awe.

"Sounds like she was a big believer," my wife said— "Ruby is reunited now too—with Jesus."

Three Summer Sons

That year, an opportunity came up for us to buy a smaller office building in Sacramento. Our three sons would be with us over the summer. I also wanted to give Elizabeth a break for her health and peace of mind. Working at our real estate firm would provide Grayson, Nolan, and Paul an opportunity to learn skills. *This will get them away from video games too*, I thought. It was a special summer working alongside them.

Nolan and Paul took turns at reception, data, tenant improvements and marketing. Grayson helped with accounting, renovation, and leasing. Our goals were to buy and remodel the building and lease it as "full-service executive office suites." Over the course of the summer we filled the office with a law firm, two accountants, tech company and counselor. There was just one space vacant.

Later at home, I said, "Things at the office are going well with the guys, but it's been all business." That weekend we went to Six Flags Amusement Park.

"Maybe we need to try and involve them in *some ministry*," Elizabeth suggested, "but how?" As usual, we prayed for an answer.

In the morning at work, several people were waiting for us in the lobby.

"We want to lease your office," they said simply.

"What's your business?" Paul asked.

Looking around at each other they smiled, and one said, "We're in the business of saving souls—we need office space for our church headquarters."

"God works fast," I laughed while relating our prayer from the night before.

All of the other tenants welcomed our new friends from *Living in God's Love Ministries*. But the local Owners Association complained in a letter that, "Your new tenant does not conform to regulations."

"What?" I exclaimed out loud, "they want us to kick out the church?"

"They want to impose a fine," Nolan added after reading over the letter—"sounds like persecution."

"Good thing you have an attorney in the office," Grayson smiled. With one letter from our lawyer, we did not hear anything further from the association.

"No news is often good news, in business," I said.

The law office manager, Richie Garlinghouse, was a close friend and Christian involved with the Union Gospel Mission. Another faith-based opportunity presented itself.

The next day we delivered food and pillows to the Mission on our way home from work.

"Our biggest need right now is pillows," director Jim had said. "It's hard to get *new* pillows."

We ended the summer celebrating with a party and us fellas playing a round of golf together. *We have our own foursome*, I thought. While strolling the links, I began to reflect back on our time together. I was so grateful for *the sons of summer*. And Elizabeth was grateful for time to recuperate!

Living in a large metro area, had often been hectic. We wanted a change of pace, closer to Paul's school. We felt called to *expand our territory*. The following month we began remodeling a Lake Village condo in Zephyr Cove, Nevada.

A New Life in Lake Tahoe

A Move to Lake Tahoe

In the fall, Nolan left for College at Simpson University. He would major in pastoral studies. We moved to Zephyr Cove in Lake Tahoe, living closer to Paul. It was hard to leave our amazing neighbors and *family of faith* in Elk Grove.

In due course, we were leading the Worship at a Church in South Lake Tahoe. The music team quickly grew from a few people to over a dozen in a very short time.

Our son Paul, as a teenager, helped with Worship at church; setting up equipment and running the projection or sound. Paul would often anticipate where the pastor was going with the sermon and place a scripture on the monitors for all to see—right before the Pastor even said the verse.

"How does he always do that?" the Pastor wondered aloud.

As Paul was in the High School chamber choir, we wanted him to join in singing on our Worship Team. But he was needed during the service to, "Help keep things running smoothly."

Late in November in Tahoe, colorful leaves were falling from the quaking aspens, and a dust of white topped the pines. We were asked to lead music for a prayer retreat at the Zephyr Point Conference Center. That day, Paul joined us singing. It was so special. Many people began dancing around to the songs: *Trees of the Field* and *David's Dance*. Paul began twirling one lady around by the arm!

Then powerful prayers were said aloud for family, the country and others. Often personal prayers spoke to the deepest places of emotional wounding.

That spring, Daughter Jennifer came to stay with us in the mountains for a few days before her move to Australia. She had a great job with a nice apartment waiting in Sydney. After the move, we were *Skyping* with her 'down under' to stay in touch. Katelyn, was traveling for an International Investment firm and living in San Francisco at the time.

With summer, our son Nolan informed us he was taking a mission trip sponsored by Simpson University, "I plan on going to Kurdistan, in Northern Iraq." Nolan said.

"Kurdistan in Iraq? Is it safe?" we wondered.

"It's time to step out of my comfort zone, I'll be okay," he said, "I'll be teaching English."

Very courageous, we thought. When God puts something on Nolan's heart, he just does it.

Arriving home Nolan shared great testimony from his trip and organized a youth retreat at our Church. Pastor Phil Fuller, from Creekside Christian in Elk Grove, came with a heartfelt message for the youth.

The following week, Nolan proposed to his college sweetheart, Amber, overlooking Lake Tahoe. Elizabeth helped Nolan make dark chocolate with white lettering that said: *"Marry Me?"*

Mountain Marriage Conference

"We make-love every night!" the blonde conference speaker said. Her husband rolled his eyes and looked at the twenty-five married couples; "Snuggling must count then," he said under his breath.

Inspired by our son's engagement, we had helped organize a marriage retreat in Tahoe, renting the Lake Village Clubhouse by our condo. Now, married folks from all over were at our first nights reception. There were appetizers and I served fancy non-alcoholic drinks.

Pastor Cejay and his wife, singer, Anna Lee, gave an engaging talk on God's design for marriage, "When the Pharisees pressed Jesus on divorce, he said, *'Haven't you read God made them male and female and the two shall become one flesh,'*" Sedric mentioned.

We ended the evening dancing with our marriage partners, by the roaring fire pit and pristine Lake Tahoe.

In the morning, we met at our Tahoe Church where Elizabeth and I shared our marriage story. I mentioned reading *Wild at Heart*, and how men are *not* to make their wives the object of the journey. "It's about having our wives come alongside us in life—they're not to be our end goal."

"Men place too much pressure on us women," my wife stated; "During my recent mastectomy surgery, Eric got the kids to school, did the laundry and he even got us out of debt. I had to be helpless and on my deathbed, before I was ready to relinquish control of the home and our finances."

"The man is also supposed to be the spiritual head-of-the house," I added, "It's not a popular message these days."

"We do work together; Elizabeth chimed in, "And pray."

"Remember—ninety-nine percent of married couples that pray together, stay together according to a Gallup Poll," I elaborated, "we try and pray together morning and night."

"We have to forgive each other our past marital trespasses," my wife finished. *Or current ones*, I laughed.

At the end of our talk, I headed to the piano and we sang our signature song: *Go in Peace—Your Sins are Forgiven.*

The Call to Maui

That fall, Elizabeth and I headed back to Hawaii for more restoration. We would work a little on our vacation property and also sing at our favorite Calvary Church there. We had received the message to; *focus more on ministry and sharing the Gospel*, so we jumped at the chance to do a little music at a Calvary Church in Maui, Hawaii. Thankfully we had saved our airline miles.

We felt called to spread the Good News through music, concerts, sharing our testimony, and worship services. We began to plan more events in Maui, Chico, Castro Valley, Santa Barbara, Europe and even in Israel!

"Maybe we can call ourselves *Musical Missionaries*," I said.

Praise Music at Calvary Chapel on the Island of Maui

Singing and Hiking in Hawaii

Arriving in Hawaii, we took the "Road to Hana." It is often referred to as *"Hana; the Journey not the destination."* One night, we stayed at the Wianapanapa cabins right on the ocean in Hana. The loud waves crashed right by our front deck. We had visited this exact spot on our honeymoon.

Early in the morning, we took the Hana Park hike towards the seven sacred pools and bamboo forest. Our goal was the 400-foot-high waterfall. Grayson, was attending the University of Hawaii in Maui, joined us. Being quite the hiker, he led the way up the long and winding Pipiwai bamboo forest trail. We felt God was leading us into new territories.

Then while traversing toward the tall ribbon of water, Elizabeth and I felt so energized that we composed and sang a new song, *"The Last Supper."* Here is a snippet of the song:

It all comes down to the last supper,
When the sky catches fire and we're called to pray...
'Forgive me Lord for I am a sinner
I receive you Jesus in my heart today
I know you died for me and rose again
Only You can take all of my sins away.'
And it all comes down to the last supper
When the sky catches fire and we're all called home,
Like the very last meal, if we don't tell a brother
The Bread of Life is right behind that door!

Once we reached the waterfall, we met a group of people from the Netherlands and started singing together! Grayson pressed pass the "danger" sign to bathe under the heavy stream of fresh water. It was exciting to engage people from other countries, singing by a remote falls named Waimoku.

We returned to Hana the next summer with son, Paul, and this time he led the waterfall hike. At the bamboo forest, we trekked along meeting new friends from India and Japan.

With Grayson at Waterfalls

201

Return to the Bamboo Forest and waterfall with son, Paul

In Hawaii we passed out more little Bibles and invited people to the outdoor church events there. The following Sunday, Pastor David Courson and his wife, Robin, asked us to join them for an upcoming tour to Israel! We would be leading singing at many holy sites around the county.

"You have been called," Pastor Courson smiled.

"Yes! We will save our pennies," we replied.

We were excited to return home because Nolan and Amber were getting married in the Apple Hill area. During their ceremony, personally written vows were touching. Over seventy friends and family members attended the blessed day.

With Nolan and Amber on blessed Wedding Day

Later, we traveled to Olympia, Washington, where our son and new daughter-in-law, had a second wonderful wedding reception. It was held at the family church and we were welcomed like long-lost relatives. We have found this love from our church families worldwide. It's like we already know them because we have the same faith in Jesus.

I Once was Blind...almost...

The way home found us staying in Klamath Falls, Oregon. Near the entry of the lakeside resort, we saw that a small *Pocket Rocket* motorcycle had crashed into the water. Coming closer, we found that the rider had died in the accident. Sadly, we heard the young man had been working at the Resort and drinking there, just minutes before his death.

I woke up in the middle of the night feeling debilitated. Suddenly, there was excruciating pain in my right eye. That week, we met with three eye doctors who had no answers.

One ophtahamologist prescribed medication for 'pink eye,' and things grew dim. Thankfully, my Father-In-Law, Dr. Bob Logan, diagnosed the eye issue in time to save my eye-sight; possibly the eye itself. I had contracted a serious case of Uveitis, or *Iritis* a bad auto-immune type of disease. *My grandfather, Mike, had a glass eyeball,* I remembered. Then my other eye developed Iritis, or traumatic inflammation of the iris. I started wearing shades.

For several weeks I had treatments short of surgery. At church, I joked with the music team, "Stevie Wonder and Ray Charles play pretty well with dark sunglasses on!"

I continued leading worship, and each week my eyes healed a little more, as others prayed over me. Over the following weeks, many faithful folks prayed for restoration.

One night, I recalled the Bible story where the Lord said to Ananias: *"Go!"* And went to where Saul was staying. Ananias placed hands upon him and said, "Brother Saul, the Lord, Jesus, who appeared to you while coming here, sent me so that *you may see again and be filled with the Holy Spirit."* Immediately, scales fell from Saul's eyes; Saul became Paul!

When Christ ASKS us to Go! We should Go! Go!! GO!!!

Shortly, by the grace of God, my vision completely healed. That month, Elizabeth and I started packing and putting together musical booklets with our favorite hymns and songs. It was time for our singing tour to Israel. We were free to head out as *Musical Missionaries!*

Called to the Holy Land

"And Jesus went up to the mountain and sent them out to proclaim the Good News…" (Mark 3:13-15)

Encountering the Majesty of Israel

In November, Elizabeth and I flew through Turkey, where we heard a commotion on the runway during a layover.

"It's just the rebels and a little firefight," a uniformed man said casually; "A small delay." We were relieved to land in Israel where we felt so much safer.

In Tel Aviv, we met our tour group at the airport. We had met the Coursons two years earlier, in Hawaii, while playing music for their Calvary Church in Maui. We were excited to be traveling to the Holy Land with such a spirit-filled couple and thirty other Christians from different parts of the world.

205

Strangely, we felt a *calling back to the Holy Land*; yet, neither of us had been there before. We would lead singing for the tour group at sites where much of the Bible happened.

Our first outing was to Caesarea along the Mediterranean Sea. It was exhilarating singing in the Roman built theatre where the Apostle Paul spoke. Pastor Courson and the men in our group gave talks at each site visited.

Later that day, we were on the top of Mt. Carmel where the prophet Elisha prayed to God, who sent a fire to consume the enemy. We were singing songs at every Holy site along the way, including a wooden boat on the Sea of Galilee.

Singing and Dancing on the Sea of Galilee

The trip took us to Syrian border by Mount Herman, "Damascus is where the fighting at the end-times will begin," our guide said prophetically, "watch for Damascus."

Our Faithful Tour Group in Israel

Temple Steps and the Wailing Wall

Pastor Courson, asked me to give a talk from the Temple steps about the "Living Waters," so we included a reenactment with Jesus at Jacobs well. Elizabeth portrayed the Samaritan woman beautifully. Then we toured the old Jewish Quarter, stopping to pray at the Western-Wailing Wall in Jerusalem.

While walking alone to the towering wall, the religious leaders began calling after me loudly. Two men in black came around a blockade after me, but I hurried to the wall. Once at the wall of prayer, I realized my head was the only one left uncovered. The "men in black" had been trying to sell me a head covering or "Yamica,"–A white round cap. By not wearing one at the wall, I was committing "a religious sin."

Then while praying, I began to see that not much had changed with "religious works"...since the Lord exposed the self-righteous Pharisees in the Temple. As I placed a simple prayer note of thanks in the wall, as is the custom, tears began to well up in my eyes. I heard a 'still small voice,' *"They were upset with me too—for telling the truth and turning over the tables. Keep talking to me...Keep praising me."* It was a very humbling and moving moment.

Afterward, we headed under the "Holy of Holies" into a large cavern and tunnel area beneath the Western Wall.

Entering the tunnel, a nice older Jewish man handed me a Yamica Cap! "This one is *free* for you," he smiled. In this kind gesture, God was working through him. Later, we visited the Holocaust Museum—a very moving experience. *Shame on anyone who denies the holocaust*, I thought.

Our tour-guide, Yuval (a Messianic Jew, or *Jew for Jesus*) inspired us with his great faith, hope and loyalty to Yeshua (Jesus) and Israel. His stories were colorful. His knowledge of history and the Bible was extensive. Yuval gave an amazing talk from the Mt. of Olives overlooking Jerusalem from the prophesy of Zechariah:

"There is no old and new testament," Yuval said. "It is all one book. Why? *Because many of the things in the Old Testament have yet to happen."* He continued, "There will be a great earthquake right below us here in the Kidron Valley, and then the Lord Jesus will come above to the temple mount."

Our hearts will always be with the Israeli people, as we learned that they are surrounded by enemies.

There are twenty-two Muslim countries around Israel. The Jews in Israel just want to live peacefully in their "Promised Land"—"We have nowhere else to go," our guide Yuval said.

When we visited Garden of Gethsemane and olive grove, David Courson suggested we each take a private walk and spend some time praying alone among the two thousand-year-old olive trees. Reaching down, I held a dark withered olive.

While praying, I thought, *many of these trees were from the time of Christ. – Maybe I'm near where Jesus sweated His own blood in prayer.* It was another powerful experience.

I would write a letter to our family and friends towards the end of our tour:

ISRAEL IS REAL! ISRAEL is AMAZING!

The people, the biblical/historical sights, the food, the weather. The stories of the Bible are coming alive for us on this remarkable trip.

Highlights were leading the music daily, and taking a wooden boat ride—singing and dancing on the Sea of Galilee, where Jesus walked on water and calmed the storm. We also went swimming in the Dead Sea where there is floating without effort, due to the 38% salt content of the water. On the trip we met the leader of *A Voice for Israel*, Hana, who gave an amazing testimony. There were deep insights into the Jewish people and culture. She asked for us to pray for, "peace in the region." All the men in the group took turns giving a talk from a related Bible verse at each Holy site visited.

A Visit to Calvary and the Garden Tomb

We wound our way through the cobble stone streets to Calvary or *Golgotha,* where Jesus was crucified. Also known as the *"Place of the Skull"* in the Bible, there was a large skull formation right in the sheer rock wall. The terrain outside the old gates of the city was rocky and desolate.

Adjacent to Golgotha was the *Rich Man's Garden* where it was spoken of that Jesus was laid in the tomb. Walking the lush green grounds, we noticed a brick winepress had been unearthed. *A Rich Man's Garden Indeed,* I thought. *How completely different from Golgotha.*

There in front of us stood a large round boulder once used to cover an open doorway. It was the Garden tomb. Scripture said the rich man had built just the one tomb for himself and then used it for Jesus. Here it was—in the whole area, only one tomb had been unearthed. One at a time we stepped inside the tomb and saw where the Lord was laid; *so ethereal.* On the back of the door was a sign saying: *"He is not here, for He has Risen!"*

Finally, our group went into a private area nearby and shared in communion together. Another moment I will not forget. Departing from our tour group was hard. We had made many new friends. As we were leaving, Yuval and Hana dubbed us, "Ambassadors for Israel to the world."

"We grow up with all of these Bible stories, but it all comes alive in the Holy Land," one man said, "You can see it, touch it and feel the presence of God all around you."

An older man, Dominic, prayed, "Lord, now that I have been to the Holy Land, I'm ready to go home to Heaven anytime you need me there!"

Arriving on the Island of Majorca Spain, we sang, *Pray for the Peace of Jerusalem*, on the crowded beach. That Sunday we drove more cobblestone streets along the ocean to the Seaside Calvary Church. The pastor was Spanish, yet felt called to preach only in English! Everyone seemed excited to hear about our trip to Israel.

Arriving back home in Tahoe, we shared our Holy Land experiences during a special service at church. With the help of son, Paul, we added photos, a video and several songs from the tour. Elizabeth reminded: *"He who blesses Israel will be blessed and he who curses Israel will be cursed."*

One Last Reunion

Our happy church reunion was short-lived when James Farmer from my old doctor band called: "Brev Creech, died from cancer, Eric—the funeral is next Saturday."

Right before we left for Israel, my old plastic surgeon friend, Brevator Creech from Chico, had called asking me to play for a special event. It would be his last musical outing.

"We're heading to Israel tomorrow to lead music," I had said. Brev knew he was dying of cancer, but had spared me the details; always thinking of others.

At the funeral for Brev, our old band sat together. An old Realtor friend, Tim Marble, sang and it was a touching event. Later, we met Doc's son, downtown, and there was a big hug. Sometimes that's all we need.

Australia

We followed up our journey to the Holy Land the following year by heading to Australia. Our daughter, Jennifer, had taken a rewarding job with "Quest." She talked us into coming one day while we were in a Tahoe blizzard. While we were snowbound, Jen was walking around on a gorgeous beach showing us the sites of her Oceanside town; via live Skype on her computer.

After the warm sun and sand of Coogee Beach called us, we reserved flights for Australia with our stockpiled airline miles. We also contacted a friend working in the Missionary field there with "YWAM" –Youth With A Mission.

Then we were all floating in the warm salty waters down under. *Ahhh~*

The boat ride to the Zoo was an adventure itself as we motored by the Sydney Opera House and sipped a delicious Ferry Cappuccino. We walked among the kangaroos, koalas, emu, and crocodiles. Jennifer was animated as our tour guide. Afterward, we wandered the cobblestone streets of the Old Sydney town that years before were inhabited by criminals, shipped there from England.

In the evening, we enjoyed dinner at the needle restaurant revolving high above Sydney; taller than the Space Needle in Seattle. The circular buffet included cucumber salad, kale medley, seafood and Caesar salad. The gals cringed while we tasted the kangaroo kabobs, emu and alligator bites.

"We were just strolling alongside these animals," I joked, "and now we're eating them."

Jennifer, a vegetarian since childhood, gave us *"The Look..."* so we offered her some of the tantalizing desserts, including napoleons, éclairs, designer cookies, chocolate dipped strawberries and gelato.

That Sunday, at a neighborhood Anglican Church by our Hotel, we shared our experience in Israel to the faithful Aussies. We also remembered to pass out "Little Bibles" to most everyone we met; hotels, restaurants, shops. No one was immune.

Everyone in the world needs a shot of 'J.C.', I said.

On our way home from down under, we stopped off in Maui and joined the worship team at First Baptist Church for the service. We shared a little testimony and sang *Go in Peace* to a hushed crowd;

> *"Jesus met a woman at someone's home one night*
> *She entered very quietly and waited out of sight*
> *she then stood by the Savior, who was about to eat*
> *the tears that trickled from her eyes*
> *she used to wash His feet – He said:*

> *"Go in Peace, your sins are forgiven,*
> *Go in Peace, you've shown great love,*
> *Go in Peace your faith has saved you,*
> *Go in Peace and Love...."*

That afternoon, we enjoyed snorkeling with the large green Hana sea turtles. The Church had a great seaside picnic and the pastor baptized someone right in the warm ocean waters.

What a beautiful creation, I thought, while viewing the rainbow of life under the waves.

We wanted to put off the flight home to freezing Tahoe as long as possible. When Elizabeth mentioned she would miss daughter Jennifer *even more than the warm weather*, I responded: "Jennifer said she's sending us a Koala Bear.'"

With Jennifer and Koala Bear in Australia

Finishing in Freedom

"You shall know the Truth and the The Truth shall set you free." (John 8:32)

After our return from Australia, we attended the annual Christmas Concert at our son Paul's High School. He was singing in their top Chamber choir. The choir director, Mr. Sonnemaker, had selected many spiritual songs, ending with Handel's Messiah. It was wonderful to hear in a public school.

Later, we shared with Son Grayson on his 25th Birthday. He was living and working in the beautiful Apple Hill area in Northern California; always willing to learn and grow.

That summer, Nolan married an amazing gal, Amber, who he met at Simpson University. They had an incredible

215

wedding in Apple Hill, with many family and friends in attendance. The Minister presiding was their Spirit-filled professor, Dr. Griffin, from Simpson University. We were not losing our son; we were gaining another beatiful daughter and her awesome family. After the honeymoon, Nolan gave his FIRST Church sermon; amazing that we can view online with many others these techy days. I know we are not supposed to boast, but I'm only human! –still have to work on that pride of course.

"On the last day, Jesus will look us over not for medals, diplomas or honors, but for our scars." -Manning

A Lion Hearted Senior named Richard

As "Musical Missionaries," we started focusing on spreading God's Love through singing and testimony. So far we had traveled to Canada, Turkey, Israel, Spain, Great Britain, Australia and then back home to the U.S.A. –where we sang in "The Carolina Bible Belt," for the first time.

Returning home to the West Coast, we visited my ninety-three-year-old Mom, Florence, at her Baywood Retirement Center. During our travels, we often find ourselves reaching out to strangers.

On our first night, we were seated with a man named Richard. He was ninety-two and new to the Baywood Community. After introductions, the conversation found its way to *faith*. Richard mentioned he grew up as a Catholic, but since WWII had not believed. Mom mentioned Dad had been at the "Battle of the Bulge."

"I was in the Battle of the Bulge too!" Richard replied with excitement.

Then, I recalled the story about Dad hearing from God to "Move his men," and narrowly escaping an attack.

"There are 'no atheists in foxholes,' my Dad would say."

"Except me," Richard replied.

I related how the thief on the cross hung next to Jesus and accepted Him at the last minute.

"Truly I tell you, today you will be with me in paradise," Jesus said.

Gazing right into his eyes I said: "Richard—you can repent and be forgiven right before you die, and still get into heaven."

By now, most of the elderly diners had left. I realized Richard had finished eating before we even sat down. He had wanted companionship.

"Do you have any family?" I asked.

"No one."

"You know, Richard, I have had a pretty wild life and if God can forgive me, he can forgive anyone," I said.

I started talking to my Mom and then overheard Elizabeth asking: "Richard would you like to accept Jesus as your Lord and Savior right now?"

"Oh, *yes* I would!"

She placed a hand over his, recalling the "sinner's prayer;" remembering a song we had written called, *The Last Supper.*

In the final strains of the song are the words below. She whispered near his hearing aid, "You can repeat this prayer after me."

"Forgive me Lord, for I am a sinner," -Richard repeated each line slowly;

> *"I accept You Jesus in my heart today,*
> *I know You died for me and rose again,*
> *Only You can take all of my sins away,*
> *Now I make You the Lord and leader of my life,*
> *In the name of our Lord Jesus Christ, Amen"*

When we were leaving, I paused and said, "I know we're going to meet again in heaven, Richard."

"Yes," he smiled, "this has been the best dinner of my whole life!"

A Final Walk in the Desert

The following morning, we said goodbye to my Mom at the senior center. We headed to Palm Desert and La Quinta, close to the border of Mexico. There we started recording a new CD of original songs at the FOSS Christian Recording Studios. The La Quinta Christian Fellowship Church had helped start this non-profit program for youth that included giving music lessons and teaching recording. We were renewed by their enthusiasm and love of God.

One day we took a walk at the Shields Date Gardens. I remembered coming there with my family, as a child, on our way to Mexico in our camper, one Christmas break.

Here we found wonderful gardens reminiscent of the Holy Land. It brought us right back to our visit in Israel.

Now at Shields in the California desert, we discovered there were statues and scenes depicting the life of Jesus.

The following Sunday, we sang at church and told the story of *Richard the Senior*, who accepted Jesus at Mom's retirement community, all by the grace of God.

After the service, we organized a large group from the church to go to brunch and take the Shields Date Garden walk with us. Along the way, we sang and took turns reading the scriptures on plaques that went along with the scenes, such as Jesus being baptized by John. Spontaneously, Elizabeth waded into the small lake to join Jesus and John in the water! Our group stayed all day until the sun began to set. It seemed we all relished remaining in these Heavenly gardens where, "God walks every evening."

Hearts Healed

That month, Elizabeth was invited to speak at the Hearts Being Healed Women's Conference in Chico. Men are not allowed in the sanctuary during the testimonies. More than three hundred women would be in attendance.

It would be hard for me returning to Chico. It was the scene of not one—but two divorces.

At the event, men are invited to help by serving food, cleaning, cooking, opening doors—but men are not allowed inside the meeting rooms. *Except,* for a most amazing time of repentance.

In the morning, the men met early to set up and prepare. Then there was a time of prayer and personal revelation with men confessing to one another. There were sixty, or so men that morning, experiencing their *own* hearts being healed. The Holy Spirit was working overtime.

One by one, while in the gym of the Evangelical Free Church, men openly repented of their sins, or the hurts they had inflicted upon women over the years. While men are sitting, the leader called out:

"Whoever has abandoned a woman, stand up—whoever has abused women verbally or physically stand up—whoever has committed adultery—had a bad divorce, assisted, approved of or driven a woman to an abortion stand up! The list seemed endless. We prayed aloud and one man repented for each sin, often through tears. By the end, every man in the room was standing.

Finally the leader asked, "Is there anything I forgot to mention?"

"Yes," one man said from the back, "Abandoning your children—you know the *Deadbeat Dad*—that's me." The husky man was weeping openly.

It cut me to the core, as I thought back to my divorces and custody battles years before. A major consequence of divorce is that children are often abandoned fifty percent of the time by each parent; sometime much more.

As the group of sixty men came around to pray and lay hands on the dad who admitted abandonment, an incredible thing took place. From the back door of the gym, a young man came running forward. It was the man's young adult son. Pushing through the crowd of men, he quickly wrapped his arms around his father.

"It's okay, Dad," the young man said, "it wasn't *all* your fault."

"Yes it was," the man cried out, "Yes it was!"

A flood of emotion fell over the group of men, as we all gathered around the father and son, and started to pray.

It reminded me of another reunion; A picture of the prodigal son returning to His Father. *This time in reverse*: The dad confessing to the son. Tears fell to the gymnasium floor. Then all the men stood in small circles and prayed over each other with anointing oil.

Then we were cued to enter the large building in two rows. Standing alongside the walls of the church, we faced away from the women. When the head of our group began to speak, the men all turned around facing the women at once.

"We are here today to repent for the devastation we men have done to you over the years; those men here today, and representing all men who have ever harmed you."

The leader called out the list of our sins: *abuse, adultery, abandonment, assisting abortion* – and those are only the "A's." One by one, men began tearing up, bowing their heads and dropping to their knees. Then women started weeping, as well. Standing up, the women spontaneously started clapping. It continued for several minutes until the last man exited the sanctuary.

Right after, Elizabeth shared her, "Tell-All Testimony," of God's love, healing, and forgiveness. During her talk, she read an excerpt from her book *Floored and Delivered* (well I had to get in a plug for her book somewhere). I snuck into the sound booth at the back of the church to help with projecting pictures of my wife's inspiring life.

At one point, during her hour-long testimony, Elizabeth reached out with forgiveness toward men; recalling the sexual abuse she endured as a child.

Even though I knew her message intimately, the Spirit of God's love was *SO* strong in that room, tears began to well up in me when my wife invited everyone to recite, *"Let us not be weary in doing good, for we will reap if we do not give up."* She had not given up. With God we had endured. *This time God helped me to stick it out and now we were blessed together.* We had hung in there through, multiple surgeries, deliverance from drinking, breast cancer, my eye disease and five children together; And four teenagers at once.

Then I heard my name being called by Elizabeth and hurried down the aisle to the nine-foot grand piano. We sang *Go in Peace,* and *I've Got a River of Life,* where our friend Tiffany joined in on guitar. After a final prayer, we had time for one more song, so we sang an impromptu version of *This Little Light of Mine*—I'm gonna let it shine. The ladies all joined in singing, like kids at summer camp.

The lights on stage were so bright I could not see any women in the room except for my beautiful wife.

In the middle of the song, I felt embraced by God's light. There was forgiveness for my past with women. Then as the song ended, Elizabeth smiled at me, and there was a moment of perfect peace. This would be the beginning of a new chapter in our lives.

One Last Dream

Right after returning from Hearts Being Healed, I had one last powerful dream:

In the dream, I was whisked away aboard a lightning express. Stepping off a transport, I joined a colorful picnic. A man greeted me dressed all in white. He was surrounded by bright rays of light and led me into a cavernous ballroom.

At the far end of the room, a dark figure sat alone at a long metal table. He was wearing a black hood and began accusing me:

"He was a womanizer, he lied and stole, he shirked his duties as a husband and father, he was a drunk and gambled—and he was full of pride."

I could only stand and take it. Looking down, I spoke quietly, "I am guilty." Everything was still.

"But I did tell them about Jesus," I managed.

Then the "Radiant One" clothed in white, put his hand on my shoulder, and said, "Don't worry, I've already taken care of this for you." He gave me a big hug and motioned for me to join the picnic outside, "they're singing," He smiled.

Suddenly, back at the picnic, I was surrounded by shining faces. My brother Daniel and my Dad were there! "I know we will meet again in heaven," I said to Dad and Dan.

"Yes!" they said joyfully, "Yes, we will."

I woke up as a beam of morning light shone through the bedroom window. I whispered to my wife, "Sweetie, I just had the most amazing dream of my entire life!"

"Then Jesus said: 'Go into all the world and tell the Good News to everyone.'" (Mark 16:15)

Traveling Musical Missionaries

"Sing to the Lord a New Song..." (Psalm 96:1)

Acknowledgments

Thanks to my amazing wife, Elizabeth Soldahl, for her unending encouragement and love. Thanks again to Sons: Grayson, Nolan and Paul, Heather, Courtney and Mom for their thoughtful input.

Thank you to my family for their love and support: In-laws Mary Ellen and Bob Logan, children: Grayson Soldahl, Nolan and Amber Soldahl, Paul McCorkle-Soldahl, daughters; Jennifer Swimley, Kate Swimley, brothers-in law: Mark Logan and Don Logan. Mother Florence Soldahl, Jerolyn Soldahl, Sister Christine, Sister Nancy and Steve Hertzog, Cousin Sue & Gary, Dan & Margo Crotty, Betty Ann, James Farmer, Steve and Mary Smith, Greg Scott & family, Christopher Melton, Bob Bohling, Bob and Nancy Gardner, Maria and Jesus Tafoya, Ian, Cathy and Angie Naef, Noble and Sharleen Spees, Greg and Darlene Scott, Dan and Margo Crotty, Kurt and Debbie Kearnes, Pastor Roger and Lois Hoffman, Daryl and Debra Fisher, Pastor Levi Thunderburk, Pastor Norm and Donna Gardner, Paul, Pastor Mark and Marie Cook, The Pappas Family, Khoi & Loan-Kim Bui, The Charvel Family, Dr. Rev. Curtis Lyons, Mitch and Melody Forrester, Pastor Sam and Joanna Shaefer, Pastor Emeritus Robert Salge, Pastor Eric and Beverly Ishimura Pastor Mark and Susan Collins, Pastor Steve and Celeste Lundblom;

We have truly appreciated the spiritual direction provided by Ministers Roger and Sandee Babcock and "Two or More Ministries," and providing prayer, truth, and wisdom

With hugs to our eternal next-door neighbors, Pastor Emeritus Rich and Karen Eddy, To St. Peter's in Elk Grove, To Pastor Phil Fuller and wife Krista, for faithful family inspiration and taking our sweet cat Purrsy! And all of my Aunts & Uncles, Cousins, Nieces, Nephews, In-laws and Great Grandmas too!

225

Bonus: A Few Healthy Tips

I believe great health is a result of a combination of faith, diet, exercise, supplements, prayer, hope, friends, family, a will to live, purpose, laughter, creativity, Christ centered meditation and mentorship.

When we rely only on science, we are showing a lack of trust in God and too much trust in medicine and ourselves. We can ask God to forgive us and ask God to help us trust Him more. *Repentance* is not a popular word; however, when we admit there is a problem, seek forgiveness and change our behavior, there is freedom. With God's help, we become free from the destructive habit. I have to work on it daily.

Here are a few tips:

- **Exercise** (my wife and I are more productive, and in better moods, on the days we exercise).

- *Avoid prescription drugs if possible!* Most have detrimental side effects including lethargy, anxiety, depression, and weight gain—which is depressing in itself. Antibiotics kill the good bacteria and are overprescribed wearing down the immune system. *Avoid Vaccines* at all costs. They may cause autism.

- **Less sugar**—sugar causes an initial "High" followed by a "Low"—hence the name, "Sugar Blues"— Less processed foods, more vegetables, salads, and fruit. Try to eat treats made with honey, stevia, or maple syrup rather than white sugar.

- **Limit alcohol** (or none at all) It *is a depressant*: *"The higher one gets at night—the Lower one feels in the morning."*

- **Laughing** and talking with friends lifts the mood.

- **20-30 Minutes of sunshine per day**, remember Vitamin D helps with depression and also may be a cancer fighter!

- **Communicate!** Get on the same page with the wife.

- **Christian counseling.** I grew up with a counselor as my father, and have attended *MANY* counseling sessions over the years. Faith-based Biblical counseling gets right to the core.

- **Singing songs of gratitude** and of God's love and mercy. Sing to Christian radio or CDs. Join a choir!

- **Walks in nature,** sports, get a massage, simplify, fellowship with others at church or Bible study.

- **Getting out of debt!** Christian Author/lecturer Dave Ramsey offers a great class and free materials online.

- **Working through parenting issues**, try the "Love and Logic" series of books, /CD's and free weekly online pointers: www.loveandlogic.com/parenting.

- **Keep a Daily Journal,** with a list of thankfulness.

- **Forgiveness**; giving or receiving; Let go and let God.

- Looking at challenges in life as *"opportunities"*: *Turn your "Mess" into a Message and "Test" into a Testimony!*

Most importantly, have *faith in God's promises*. He promises to, "restore your health and heal your wounds," "by His stripes we are/were healed," and "Your faith has made you well." We need to believe and receive these promises.

- *Finally (and I can't stress this enough)* ***DRINK WATER!***

Remember that 'Jesus is the living water and bread of life!'

Eric's Recommended Reading list:

1. New Spirit Filled Life Bible; New King James Version.
2. The Return of the Prodigal, Henri Nouwen
3. Mere Christianity, C.S. Lewis (everything by C.S. Lewis)
4. Boundaries, Townsend and Cloud ~ all Boundary Books.
5. All of Grace, Charles H. Spurgeon
6. The Greatest Fight in the World, Charles H. Spurgeon (his final manifesto)
7. The Greatest Salesmen in the World, Og Mandino
8. Wild at Heart, John Eldredge
9. Safely Home, Randy Alcorn
10. The Nine Personality Types- Wagele & Baron
11. Love and Logic Parenting, (all books), Cline & Fay
12. The Trouble with Truth, *Balancing Truth & Grace*, Renfroe
13. The Road Less Travelled, Scott Peck
14. People of the Lie, Scott Peck
15. The Man in the Mirror, Patrick M. Morley
16. Dead Doctors Don't Lie, Joel, D. Wallach & Dr. Ma Lan
17. God's Way to Ultimate Health, Malkmus & Dye
18. Becoming a Contagious Christian, Mittelberg, Strobel
19. The Prayer of Jabez/Secrets of the Vine, Bruce Wilkinson
20. Floored and Delivered, Elizabeth Soldahl, Spiritual Firepower - *Unleashed* Eric Soldahl
21. Financial Peace/ Total Money Makeover, Dave Ramsey
22. Surviving the Prodigal Years, Marcia Mitchell
23. Biblical Eldership, An *Urgent Call* to Restore Church Leadership, Alexander Strauch
24. Living in God's Love / Just as I am, / Christian Worker's Handbook, Billy Graham

25. Celebration of Discipline/Prayer, Richard Foster
26. The Divine Conspiracy: Rediscovering Our Hidden Life in God, Dallas Willard
27. Sailing Around the World, Captain Joshua Slocum

Discography *(to name a few)*

1. *Christmas Time in my Town*, a Collection of original Christmas songs, ©1989 Scott, Soldahl & Kearnes

2. *When Love is Strong*, Members Only Band *CD*, ©1990, And *Live from KFM*, ©1992

3. *Maxwell, Mundi & Soul*, Originals Cloud 9 studios, ©2001

4. *Tropix Jazz*, An eclectic Tropical & Latin mix, *CD*, ©2002

5. *When Sunday Comes*, *CD* of original faith songs, ©2002

6. *Grace Notes from the Piano Room*, original compositions, ©2009 & ©2010

7. *The I Believe & Lovestock Concert CD's* ©2011, ©2012

9. *The Lost Tapes, from Windfall*…online…

10. Ammin City Jammin Band, Part 1, YouTube

11. Faith on Fire Original Videos on YouTube and

11. *Go In Peace album*, a collection of original faith songs, © 2018, E&E Soldahl. All Songs, *Dovestar Music International*

If you enjoyed my story please consider leaving a review; **Direct link at:** **http://www.amazon.com/dp/1732024626**

Post Script

Eric Soldahl is a music director, writer and entrepreneur. Along with his wife, Elizabeth they travel as Musical Missionaries, giving testimony with original music at concerts, conferences, and churches. They have five children together. Based in the Sierra Nevada mountain area, they also enjoy hiking, biking, golfing, composing, remodeling and studying the Word of God. Missions are planned for every continent, "to spread the loving message of salvation through Jesus."

For more information on Eric and Elizabeth's Music and Missionary Ministry go to: ***www.Faithonfire.net***

A Prayer of Redemption

Dear Lord Jesus, I know that I am a sinner, and I ask for Your forgiveness. I believe You died for my sins and rose from the dead. I turn from my sins and invite You to come into my heart and life. I want to trust and follow You as my Lord, Savior and friend. In Jesus Name. Amen.

Made in the USA
Columbia, SC
14 December 2018